Crucifixion and Resurrection
The Rhythms of Life

Poet, Madman, Mystic

Autobiography of a Poet in Poetry

The Phoenix Trilogy
Book I

Daylight Publishing　　　　　　　　　　　　　　　　　　　　**Roy. E. Day Jr.**
With Lulu Publishing
　　　　　　Edited and Cover by Helen Manget

Dedication

To my parents, especially thank to my father for his financial support of this project, siblings and their children, my friends, cousins, spiritual teachers and to this beautiful planet, our Mother Earth.

Introduction

This three book autobiography in poetry covers the first forty years of my life, with the poetry starting at seventeen. I have attempted to make it primarily poetry, but have supplied enough prose to provide context for the interested. It was collected and first edited in 1994 and although published years later the original time frame, attitude, and perspective was retained.

Table of Contents

Part I 1971-1972 — 5

- Disney Girl — 9
- Also A Lover — 10
- Golden Field — 11
- Hypothetical — 33
- Poet of Conflict — 35
- Battles Are Fought — 36
- Jesus - When? — 39
- The Pig Poem — 45
- Awkward God — 47
- Strength — 52

Part II 1973-1974 — 53

- Don't Want Sympathy - Picnic in Hell — 53
- Christ Keeps Climbing Down — 60
- One Inside — 64
- Held His Own — 66
- Jesus' Lady — 67
- Little Things — 69

Part III 1974-1975 — 70

- Exoteric Exclusion — 74
- Write Our Character — 78
- Paradox — 79
- Self-Responsibility — 80
- Moral Evolution — 81
- Inconsistent — 82
- Seen the Light — 83
- Know I Don't Know — 84
- The White, the Light — 85
- The Only Creature — 86
- Edge of the Known — 88
- Vibrant Celebration — 90
- Beauty and the Beast — 93

To the Young Man Spending all his Time _____ 95
Chasing Physical Gratification _____ 95
Communication _____ 96
She Is Not Gone _____ 98
She said I Love You _____ 100
Susan Is Gone _____ 102
Starts her Searching _____ 104
Different _____ 106
Two So Young _____ 107
Middle Aged Doldrums _____ 108
Alone _____ 110
Today's Children _____ 111
Nixon & Company _____ 112
Tijuana Blues _____ 113
Strong and Brave _____ 116
Dominion? _____ 117
Nature's Children _____ 119
Overwhelmed _____ 121
God Gave _____ 122
Spring _____ 125

Part IV 1976-1979 _____ *133*

Damn Deceiver _____ 138
Sweet Smiling Woman _____ 140
We Could Be _____ 141
Ocean of Our Love _____ 142
Illusions Shattered _____ 143
Dreams of Rings Shattered _____ 144
Beauty at Sunrise _____ 147
All That I Wanted _____ 149
It's a Damn Shame _____ 151
Métis Shamanism and Sweatlodge Christianity _____ 155
Grandfather Eagle _____ 159
Try to Justify _____ 161
Why Have You Stopped It _____ 166
Jesus in a Dream _____ 169

Wanted Gift	171
Please Be With Me	172
Good Omens	175
Hawk and Butterfly	176
Like Thunder	177
Be Blessed	179
I Spit on Progress	180
The New Revolution	184
Thy Will be Done	186
The Waking Dream	188
Base of the Pyramid	189

Part V 1979-1982 — *190*

Quit Asking	191
Ain't the Point	192
I'd Never Seen	193
The Question	194
Perfect Lover	195
Now Is Forever	197
Once More Found	198
Mystery of the Goddess	199
So Mean	200
I Step Willingly Into the Darkness	203
One Hundred Hunters	205
Stop the Wind	207
Queen of Hearts	209
Butterfly Flying Free	210
Strong and Silent	211
Newness Fades	211
Hold on to the Future	212
Stuffed Monkey	213
Dark Stage Passing	214
Stopped Feeling Young	217
Just Like Them	219
Child of Freedom	221
C - Section of the Soul	222

Part I 1971-1972

Everyone has their own ways of dealing with the stresses and hardships inherent in Life. One of mine has been writing poetry; which I have done prolifically since I was thirteen. It was not so much a conscious choice as a necessity, a tool of adjustment; giving voice to subconscious thoughts and feelings raging within me. This behavior of writing poetry, first spurred by the irrational and unconscious forces loosened by puberty and adolescence, has continued throughout my life. Whether as a psychological adjustment, a statement of unconscious thoughts and feelings, or ideas and possible solutions bubbling up from a deeper and more intuitive level of knowing, the poetry continues.

As I reviewed over twenty years of poetry, I found my poetry fit into five general categories of subject matter. There are poems dealing with: family and friends; romance and relationships; historical, political, and social commentary; religious, mystical, and metaphysical commentary; and what I call Earthsongs or Goddessongs about the inspiration and beauty found in Nature.

These poems tell the story of my life and somewhat reflect my generation. Although some might think such work would be too personal to be of general interest, I have found that **if a poem is good and true other people will be able to relate and project their own experiences into the words, finding their own meanings.**

Since the poems in this volume are presented in chronological order, the reader not interested in the biographical aspect of this work may want to skip around to find poems that are of personal interest. Not everyone is interested in the love life of a teenager in '72.

The reader should be warned because of the honest and revealing nature of the work the author is not always presented in the best light and admittedly at times as an adult my behavior was despicable. Hopefully the reader will reserve judgment, believe in redemption, and feel more favorable towards me by the end.

This first book of my poetic biography begins with my senior year in high school, my graduation and first forays out into the larger world, the tragedy that was to dramatically change so much of my life, and my adaptation and continuation. The second book is a love story told in the poetry written during the course of the relationship. The third is a more conventional collection of poems.

Although the poetry flowed since the early teens the first attempt at collecting and organizing my poetry was an untitled fifty page effort for a brown haired beauty named Wendy. Beginning in the tenth grade I went through a series of relationships of various lengths and depths; there was Merrimeth, Alocye, Michelle, Lynda, and Michael (spelled like the male name) before I settled down with my serious high school relationship, Peggy. She was a year younger; a quiet, pretty girl who longed for her dead father and endured her "functional alcoholic" mother. I came with a large, loud, loving family and Peggy was attracted to my home life which provided her with something she didn't get at home. We had a sometimes good, sometimes firery and tempestuous relationship; we behaved like teenagers; we broke up, we got back together. I was immature, jealous, possessive. There was a difference in lifestyles, I partied harder, she was more reserved.

Approaching graduation I experienced the ambivalent feelings of loving her, but also wanting to experience a variety of relationships, to fully experience that wild freedom which is the prerogative of youth. This is a common enough paradox experienced by young people, the desire for a real and full relationship providing commitment and security, in conflict with the natural desire for freedom and a variety of new romantic experiences. Peggy felt this dichotomy as well and we went through various off and on phases. She began high school as a well-liked petite cheerleader who went counter culture as the years went by and she never lacked admirers. During one of our off phases, while still feeling love for Peggy, I fell "in love" with Wendy. She was a somewhat troubled cheerleader with a distant mother and a bigot father who secretly belonged to a racist organization. He owned a well known business that advertised on TV a lot.

He made money selling discount furniture to poor people on credit and drove a flashy corvette. After his daughter disobeyed him for "the first time ever" he picked me up in that 'vette with a loaded .38 revolver on the dash and threatened to end my life via a contract killing which he claimed would cost him two thousand dollars. Many years later he took his own life, possibly with that same handgun.

Many kids experience high school as a best of times/worst of times situation and we were no different. One aspect of the good side was that I'd been lucky enough to have been elected senior class president. I wasn't the most popular kid in school or anything; just an advocate of democracy and student autonomy probably best known as the captain and MVP of the soccer team. Part of the not so good part was going through much of my senior year with two girlfriends. It was not a comfortable situation, both girls were juniors, and one quarter even had a class together. The emotional conflict and turmoil of this situation resulted in the Wendy poems. It is easy for adults to think that kids at sixteen and seventeen are just immature children; and they very well may be. But that in no way diminishes the intensity and sincerity of the emotions they feel and the behavior they display. Literature's most famous lovers, Romeo and Juliet, were several years younger than we were at the time. I'd been writing poetry for four years, but this situation generated enough to start compiling, collecting, and editing them.

Of course, there was more going on than just romance. Looking back I especially remember the years 1968 through 1973 as wild times to be young and free in America; but for some Americans, they were dangerous, deadly times.

My senior year was 1971-72; social and sexual revolutions were under way, expansion of consciousness and the search for meaning were popular topics, and what had started as a dirty little war in Southeast Asia was using up body bags and American flags at a horrific rate. My cousin did two tours "in country" with military intelligence and told me with disgust the politicians would not let us fight to win. People were fighting and dying over there, back here there was social revolution; a kind of chaos and raw energy were palpable in the streets.

Following are four of the Wendy poems, they are representative of the times as well as the relationship, its conflicts, and uncertainties. The reader must remember how young I was; although like most teenagers I felt I was very mature for my age, in retrospect I can accept the possibility that I might not have been as mature as I thought, both as a person and a poet. This book, hopefully, shows my growth and evolution. I'll begin with a rambling poem inspired by a Beach Boys song.

Disney Girl

I felt like writing
I don't know what
but I hear "our song"
about country shade
and lemonade
and a turned back world
and a local girl
and the things we like
and a peaceful life
with a forever wife
and a kid some day.

Well, Disney Girl
with our fantasy world
Am I coming back?

I'll leave you alone now

and make your life easier
but is it a fantasy world
and are you a Disney Girl
and will you be coming back?
Back to our fantasy world
with my Disney Girl
will you be coming back?

Also A Lover

How can you tell me
now I'll finally be happy?
How can you tell me
happiness will end my search?
How can you express
the finality you did in your letter?
How can you tell me
to hurt you was my intention?
What's wrong with a dream world
if God is your biggest fantasy?
How can we leave each other
if we are a part of each other?
How can you say you're selfish
when it's me who keeps holding on?
How can you say thank-you,

when you just looked into a mirror?
How can you collect your thoughts about me
when emotions are so irrational?
How can you be the things you list
without also being a lover?

Golden Field

For what it's worth
the stuff you wrote
is worth very little
except to show
you're all pissed off

You ask questions
that we've both asked
and answered nothing
as we've both done.
But you're overlooking
that you think of me
when you're alone
as I do you.

You're asking me
just what the hell I'm doing

right now, accepting you
accepting you
as you accept me.
And that's all that matters
about that, at least.

I'm not a fool
I'm not a god
I'm not Stalin
I'm not Prince Charming
I'm not your brother
(though maybe similar)
I'm me, just me
and you accept me
or you don't
but you do,
or else it's all useless.

I don't know me
but this, this I know,
I don't have God,
but I must have honor
whose requirement is quality
a quality of life
that makes me

accept me

as hopefully you do.

This quality of life

I must attain

to be satisfied

and to satisfy you,

though I'll do it for me

purely for me

to be satisfied

and honorable.

Here I am

again

writing to you

and thinking

thinking

about days in a field

and a natural look

in your eyes

with no "faces"

just us alone

together.

With no people around

we did great

so...

so...
I miss your smile
when I'm alone
and you are too
because actions
then
were touches
and glances
and gazing
and gazing
between eyes
and arms
around bodies
that never touched
like they might have
with different owners.
But we did enough
with one person leading the way
unsure of what
the responses meant.

But a hug
and a touch
was enough
more now

than a thousand tears
I cry every day
on the inside.
Others cry on the outside
I'm past that now.

Now
actions are words
that await actions
unsuccessfully?

A long time
a long time ago
I told you
I wouldn't try
to run your life
and I won't
unless I'm mad
and then I act with words
like now.

I didn't use to
but I read that I was wrong
but God wouldn't tell me
TV did.

By now you're probably quite confused

quite confused

But I'm straight

and there is

there is a message

here

somewhere

somewhere, from heart to hand

a poem or image forms

with a soul

somewhere within

between two worlds

both

of happiness

of sorrow

alone

surrounded

dead.

God knows

if there is one

God knows.

This poem

if that is

what this is
may "break a record"
records
records
we broke
some records
You and I.

I remember, but I'm tired
I'm tired
I'm eighty years old
I'm only twelve
I'm tired
I'm tired
of being torn
with no actions
and no changes
and words
and tears
from those
I must not know
Do I
Do I know
Do I know you?
Do I?

But I don't mind
really, I don't.

It is sad
though
when you think
or remember
good times
that could have been better
but were good enough
for all concerned
and still
maybe could be.
I don't know.
I'm a tired old man
I'm a seven year old
in love
or the world's
most renowned cynic
God knows,
God knows
maybe
or at least TV
it can tell you
what to do

I could tell it
where to go.

Who knows
God might be there too
or maybe
God and Stalin
are having Peace Talks
Peace Talks
in Paris France
in a TV
around a table
or maybe
Roy and Peggy
will get married
to Wendy
and have their own little Vietnam
and love could go
all around
and maybe
and maybe
catch my mind.

God knows,
maybe

5 to 2 in the 2nd
4 to 3 in the 3rd
God over Satan in the 5th
suicide over life in the last.
Faces over Nature
glances over tears
hugs over frowns
and God's in his heaven
and all's wrong with the world
which is only right
only right.
God knows
maybe
maybe
maybe I love you
maybe
maybe I hate you
maybe
Maybe God knows
maybe
if not, TV's our man

But do you
do you remember
rolling and fighting

fighting with love

in the fields

and loving

with fights

in the fields.

maybe, maybe

but then

at least

I acted

made actions

I mean

"I mean"

and other jokes

that weren't even funny

to us

anymore.

Maybe TV knows

maybe

if not

God knows

maybe.

It could be a first

"a first".

How would you like

a used mind
good for nothing
or a used love
good for -
you?
maybe
maybe
words are easy
feelings make actions
actions
actions of love:
glances, hugs,
fighting with affection
affection
I gave
you received
you talked
and thought affection
I gave
I touched
YOU
You made faces
at others
I cried on the inside
I loved

on the outside.
You talked
on the outside
loved
maybe
maybe, on the inside
maybe, maybe
but, do you remember
a golden field
and a football tackle
and a kiss
and a bridge
between eyes
that couldn't
or shouldn't
ever be broken
and maybe
maybe hasn't been
or ever will be
maybe.
God knows
maybe
maybe TV knows
maybe
I don't.

Somewhere
between the hand
and the heart
is a broken soul
somewhere
God knows
maybe
do you
do you
do you?
Am I really crazy?
or do I
could I
really ever be
capable
capable of love
love
love
Do you?
Words
words are easy
for you
actions aren't

faces are

Are you a face

a face for me

is it real

or one of many

or was it the real one

you saved for me

except for Joe

" Go blow, Joe Schmoe"

a child's book

for the seven year old

in love

that I am

or the crazy-ass

I am

searching

searching

searching for God, truth, love

and a face

a true one

a constant one

from you

to me

and to the rest

to go to hell.

But I'm an eighty year old cynic
God, truth, love - suck
so I'm a seventeen year old
who doesn't know his ass
from his nose
but knew a virgin from a whore
and used to do the same
to both.
But do you
do you remember
a golden field
and a tackle
and a kiss
and a hug
and four eyes meeting
and acting
like tears never could
or would
if they're fake.
I don't know
neither does God
maybe, maybe TV
or you
or Satan
sitting around a TV

in Paris France
buying fashions
that you wear
after 40 deep knee bends.

I can see now
the thousands
thousands of faces
you'll make reading this
which one
is supposed
to make me
feel stupid
or inferior
or loved
or stupid
or both
or maybe
maybe God
maybe God knows.
Maybe
make a face
the one for me
shed a tear
if you please

say you love me
if you care
show you love me
if you dare
make a face
it's all the same
all the same
all the same.
But I don't feel
stupid
don't feel
inferior
don't feel
loved
or even d
(All of the above).
Maybe
maybe
maybe God knows
maybe
but you know
I don't feel crazy
just tired
loved too much
loved too little

a seven year old

an eighty year old

or a boy

with a beautiful

a beautiful

a so-beautiful-to-me girl

with a boy - me

in a golden field

with love

love

I felt real love

real, I thought

like the tears

coming out

now

now

usually on the inside

now, on the outside

and down

1-2-3-4-5-6-7-8-9-10

knock-out

but guess what

they went back.

Well, do you remember

I do

I loved

very much

very much

but I'm always

always torn

and never know

where

or how

to go to hell

or heaven

or which is around a TV

in Paris France

or in a golden field

with a beautiful girl

and a crazy boy

who loved too much

too many

and hates too much

so many

maybe, maybe God knows

maybe

do you

well, do you?

I don't.

But do you remember

a golden field
and a tackle
and a hug
and a kiss
and eyes meeting
and reflecting love
love
love, beautiful girl
do you
do you love
or do you act
like actors, not actions.
This poem
means nothing
means everything
reflects nothing
reflects love
love
do you
do you love
can you act
make a face
cry a tear
one for me
not Jim

give me a scowl

for Gary

give me a memory for Joe

give me a tear

a tear will do

but do you

do you love

or can you act

like actions

or can you

make a face

one face

and make it your true face

the right one

the one that a fool

who is seven

or eighty

might love

if

if you act

in actions

and love

and live with one face

that makes no one feel

inferior or stupid

but can make me

only me

feel loved

feel loved

by you.

Hypothetical

I've got to slow my mind down

from thinking, to this medium

Because I've got to try to be honest

even if it doesn't benefit me

I told you I was free from her

now I'm even free-er

And I told you long ago

that my relationship with her

Didn't affect ours

I think I meant that

But you should know

I've told her I love her

And if we were three years older

that I would marry her.

If I was from a small town

like our cousins

I might have married her this year,

but while being hypothetical

If we were in a small town
I might have married you.

As previously mentioned, and as is so often the case with youth, my senior year, was both the best and worst of times. There was plenty of emotional conflict and hurt, but it was also a fun, chaotic, wonderful year. So after a year of high times and "women problems" my best friend, Tom, and I decided to do the *Easy Rider* trip and go on a hitchhiking tour of America; which the younger reader should know was much safer and more common that it is today. Hitchhiking and picking up hitchhikers was just a part of the times for a large segment of society. Now, one thinks of the homeless and ex-cons when thinking about hitchhiking.

Our first goal was Daytona Beach, Florida. Our second goal was to come home and play in an amateur soccer championship. Our third goal was California, via our thumbs and the U.S. highway system. As we started out on this odyssey, I kept a journal and continued to write poetry, much of which reflected my youthful appreciation for the artistic aesthetics of the less joyous side of life.

In the same way that the ancient Greeks loved their tragedies, and the Japanese folk heroes are often failures or martyrs by Western standards, I had come to appreciate the aesthetic beauty and the creative impetus of emotional conflict, pain, and chaos. Many of the poems from this period express this appreciation of the beauty often found in human tragedy, chaos, and conflict. They sometimes also betray my age and the arrogance of youth.

Poet of Conflict

I am a poet of conflict
not much more
The beauty I describe
is the ecstasy of anguish
The passion of sorrow
the chains and choices
Of wanton lust and emotional combat.

In a time of peace
such as this
With little here to care about
or worry over
It is hard for me
to be creative
Although the inspirations here
to others
Would be enormous.

I am a poet of conflict
although joy
May find a page or two of mine
written in her honor
It will be the joy
Of a conflicting resolution
While waiting darkly in the shadows
Lies another.

Battles Are Fought

I am not a poet of Nature's beauty
except on rare occasions
I am not a poet of God's love
and I doubt I ever will be
But when a woman leaves her man
or a man has too many lovers
That's where bards like me come in
the poets of conflict
and not just conflicts of the heart
but the battles which stir
within out natures, within our souls
which bring people together
or tear them apart
which bring tears from the strong
or strength from the weak
It is the overcoming of hardships
and the way the battles are fought
which makes Life, for me
beautiful and real.

One more poem from Daytona represents the spiritual conflicts I felt at the time. At seventeen I was concerned with the search for meaning, for truth, for God. I had been raised in the Southern Baptist denomination, although we attended (in relation to Southern Baptists) an urban, liberal church, not a conservative "hellfire and damnation" church as is so often associated with the Southern Baptists. I had grown up regularly attending Sunday school and church, but even as a small child I felt many conflicts with the brand of Christianity I was being taught.

Although my father was active in the church and later became a deacon, my mother was and still is an agnostic. We five children were raised by both parents to think for ourselves and not to be sheep-like blind and unthinking followers. So at an early age I came into disagreement with certain aspects of protestant Christianity. I accepted what Jesus taught, that God is Love; but found much in what I was being taught illogical and inconsistent with the "God is Love" premise. It did not seem logical that a God of Love would eternally punish or reward souls throughout infinity - millions and millions of years - for the actions and transgressions of one short lifetime. What is 75 years in comparison to eternity? It seemed a God of Love and a God of laws was bound to have a better plan than that. In Sunday school they taught us, even as small children, that the un-baptized would go to Hell forever. A logical God of Love would not damn an Eskimo, or a Pygmy, or an aboriginal Bushman who was good and wise and loving, to Hell forever just because they weren't converted to a foreign and alien religion that many had never heard of. That would be inconsistent with the concept that God is Love.

The wishful and childlike idea that man has been given dominion over

Nature is refuted constantly by hurricanes, earthquakes, tsunamis, and floods. It is easy to believe that as the self-conscious thinking creatures on this planet we should accept our husbandry to Mother Earth and work harmoniously with Nature for the betterment of all Life. Husbandry is believable; dominion is constantly refuted by Nature's un-controllable might.

Maturing in age I also noticed that Christianity seemed to devalue women, to portray them unfavorably in general, from Eve on, and to downgrade the sacred feminine aspect which gives birth to Life throughout Nature. The picture of women in the Bible was all too often that of temptresses; the idea that sex and procreation was something inherently shameful never set right with me.

Even as a small child I had always intuitively felt that **Nature is God's beauty in manifestation.** The Universe is God's physical body. It always seemed to me that churches should be built to accent the beauty of Nature which God had so graciously given humanity to enjoy. Instead churches are often huge walled buildings with the windows stained so that Nature seems locked out, deemed unwanted or unaesthetic. This seemed to me to symbolize that such institutionalized religions were a sterilized, intellectual man-made construct attempting to establish a link between humanity and Divinity with the rest of God's creation ignored and excluded.

Despite these reservations, I found the life of Jesus, his birth, ministry, and sacrifice to be inspiring, and his message of love and forgiveness rang true on an intuitive level. Yet I couldn't help but be curious why so many supposed Christians, especially evangelists and ministers were conspicuously wealthy, drove luxury cars and lived in expensive homes when Jesus clearly and unequivocally had told his wealthy followers to sell their excess, share with the poor, and follow him. Growing up I wondered why our church had no members of color yet employed black janitors. I wondered how many <u>real</u> Christians there were who actually followed what Jesus taught. How many churches operate the way the original Christians churches did? These questions and my natural skepticism are reflected in the following Daytona poem written after being approached by Jesus freaks, a situation that reminded me of an Elton John song.

Jesus - When?

Jesus, was he but a man
Jesus, scribbled in the sand
Jesus, was he God or man
Jesus, are you gonna set me free me
Jesus, when will I be free

Last night I drew in the sand
Last night, I asked Jesus in
Last night, I queried, God or man
but Jesus didn't set me free
Jesus, he didn't set <u>me</u> free

Jesus freaks, out in the street, telling me to praise
Praise God for all the good around

Blame man for all the bad
when is Jesus gonna set us free
when is he gonna let us all be free

"Jesus freaks, out in the streets
Handing tickets out for God"
They told me that he loved me
I told them thanks anyway
But it's a little hard to believe
Jesus, when you gonna set us free
Jesus, when you gonna let us all be free?

The next poem is called the pig poem and reflects my anger, animosity, and outrage at the hypocrisies of the times. Indeed, I believe that mass outrage at obvious and blatant societal hypocrisy was one of the instigating factors of the social and sexual revolutions of the late sixties and early seventies. As I matured I have grown in my understanding for the necessity of law enforcement and my appreciation for those who serve; as does almost anyone who has ever run a small business. My martial arts sifu is ex-law enforcement, and I have friends who are police or with other enforcement agencies and I don't want them to be offended by this poem; it is just how I felt at the time.

At seventeen. I was no angel, and had experienced a few interactions with law enforcement. During some everything was the way it should be, but in one situation that did not result in arrest I was struck in the groin while not offering resistance, in the least. It was no big deal; as someone who had played organized soccer, basketball, and football from age nine to thirteen, I'd been hit in the testicles before. But usually it was accidental. Also I'd witnessed police officers refuse to render aid when a teenager was choking on her own vomit. I had to get down on the floor next to her, turn her head sideways, put my fingers in her throat and remove vomit so she could breathe. To this day she credits me with saving her life. When asked, before I took action, if they were going to do anything to help the police officers said they hadn't received first aid training, that it wasn't there job. Their apathy and contempt for someone in need of aid had horrified me. So at seventeen I knew there were good cops and bad cops, good laws and bad laws.
You will never meet anyone who is more against real crime than myself. I hate

theft, rape, murder; (with the exception of war) there is no justification for causing hurt and pain to another except self-defense. But I separate such victim-involved behavior from issues dealing with alcohol and drug abuse. Unless that abuse leads to the harm of someone else, I would keep victimless offenders separate from real criminals using something similar to the Amsterdam model. Think of how different the homeless issue would be if we had a strong national mental health department/program that dealt with mental health, addiction, drug abuse, and alcohol abuse in an aggressive but humane, rational, and common sense manner. There might not be a homeless problem like we face today. Many countries in Europe with strong mental health programs don't have a homeless problem at all. Their mentally ill are being treated, not left to wander the streets and fend for themselves, leaving parts of our large cities smelling like urinals.

As the story is recounted, remember it was 1972, right after a popular phrase summed up an attitude for many: "turn on, tune in, drop out." But we were nothing that extreme, we were just regular kids from the suburbs. Coming back from Daytona our ride home missed a turn in the middle of the night and our path back took us through the <u>then</u> (and I emphasize then) notoriously corrupt little corner of hell in southeast Georgia known as Waycross. Tom, myself, and our ride, Mark were pulled over by eight police cars some time after midnight for having long hair and out-of-county license plates. Police cars came out of everywhere, men aiming guns at us came running up at us screaming. It was a lot of fire power for the offense of being young long-hairs from the city.

They very possibly planted or legitimately found a roach inside a tennis shoe on the floorboard, then tore our car and backpacks apart, coming up with some herb and one single hit of mescaline, and one single hit of speed. We were screwed.

Immediately after our arrest on the way to jail Mark joked that whoever found his traveler's checks was in for a good time. The two plain clothes cops driving took his joking remark as a personal insult, pulled the car over and stopped in the dark, on some side street in the middle of nothing and told us to get out of the car. Handcuffed, we held on to each other in the back seat and Mark said he was sorry, profusely. We all said he was sorry. Repeated and profusely. We were scared shitless and not afraid to show it. If we had gotten out of that car, we may have never gotten back in, or been heard from again. During that time period in the Deep South it was not unheard of for blacks and hippies to disappear without a trace, or to get shot and killed while "attempting" to escape police custody, or to be found hanging as a "suicide" in jail. Down there in Ware County sometimes blacks and hippies just disappeared. In the swamp. Gator meat. Once they decided we weren't going to give them any excuse to do us damage, they got back in the car and we continued on to jail.

They joked about how they were going to help a friend paint his house that weekend. One of them said laughingly, that after a couple of six packs he'd paint bananas on the walls, he wouldn't care. To them, this was hilarious as well as legal, but a little reefer and a hit of mesc and our lives seemed ruined. As they transported us to jail in an unmarked, undercover car during the early morning hours they kept recklessly running red lights and stop signs. Nobody was in any hurry, they simply believed they <u>were</u> the law, so they didn't have to obey it.

In their defense, things could have gone much worse than they did; much, much worse. They started to put the three of us in the city of Waycross holding cell/drunk tank on a Friday night. It was full of inebriated, angry red-necks who looked at us three young longhairs like a pack of lions looks at a herd of antelope. As they walked us from processing to the holding cells the cops were laughing about a fight that had just occurred in which a troublesome inmate had taken an ass whipping that they had thoroughly enjoyed. Fifteen to twenty pissed-off red-necks could have done the three of us serious bodily harm and from their facial expressions had every intention of doing so. One of the deputies had unlocked the door and was putting us inside when possible lawsuit must have flashed through his mind and he asked us how old we were. I hurriedly answered I was seventeen - still a minor, so they put all three of us in a separate cell. That saved us from almost certain violence and possibly serious injury.

The next day they moved us to the Ware County jail, where they treated us well enough and the food was great. Since at that early point in my life I had no standard for comparison of jail-house cuisine, I had no idea just how good their food really was. I still remember their sweet cornbread with fondness.

One comic event did make our incarceration more tolerable. Mark's father was a PR man who worked with politicians around the state. One of the local politicians came to visit Mark on our second day inside. Before he arrived some of the police put on their dress uniforms and were waiting out front for the (state) senator to arrive. Mark "hocked a lugee" through two sets of steel bars, out a window, over a ledge, directly on top of one of the cops dress hats. We rolled on the floor, clutching our sides laughing, while the cop looked up and figured himself assaulted by an over-flying bird. That and flushing some herb they didn't find down the toilet were our only two moments of respite. The rest was pretty awful. My parents thought a few days in jail might teach me a needed lesson. Three days and ten thousand dollars bail later and I was out, charged with two felonies and a misdemeanor. "Do not pass go. Do not collect 200 dollars."

You haven't committed physical harm or injury to anybody (except possibly yourself), but you are screwed.

The Pig Poem

According to the pigs I talked to
the drugs, they're only going to hurt me
but if I'm not old enough to decide
if I should hurt myself that way or not
then how come I'm old enough
to pay the price that others do
for <u>really</u> hurting people

How come if I'm convicted and I tell someone I want a job
I might as well have raped a grandmother

as have the dope that was in our car

I wonder why I can't hurt myself in private
or why I have to pay in public
or why the pigs can drink but I can't smoke
or why they run through all the stop signs and red lights taking us to jail
when they're in no hurry, and neither are we
why do they break the laws
that they're supposed to enforce

but they wear the badge of law - it protects them
I wear the tag of felon - it condemns me.

The whole court/sentencing process took a long time. The judge told us he had previously let young men go into the military instead of dealing with the legal system but they had recently complaints and had discontinued the practice. Eventually, the result of our missed turn in the middle of the night was pleading guilty, paying a fine, and a two years sentence to be served on probation. However, so many politician's sons and daughters were in the same boat we were in, someone in surprising wisdom had authored and passed our state's "first offender act". We qualified for it and gladly took it. If we did everything we were supposed to and completed our probation without incident, our record would be expunged.

I turned eighteen a convicted double felon on probation. My cousin, just back from Viet Nam said under no condition should I think about joining the service as a solution to my current problems. He said that even if I lied about my legal status and got in, after basic training and specialized training I'd be in Nam just in time for the fall of Saigon. He was in military intelligence, he knew, and he was exactly right.

Our U.S. soldiers never lost a single conventional battle in Viet Nam but our fucking politicians managed to lose the war. Viet Nam fell and went communist but the other dominos did not fall as the pretentious pundits had predicted with their "domino theory". Such is history.

To make a long story short, the only jobs available to convicted double felons in Atlanta in 1972 where high-danger, low paying jobs like demolition work. Months after getting into demolition work I fell the distance of seven stories, around 150 feet in a demolition mishap which claimed two lives.

Awkward God

On October 28, 1972
I was lifted by a 150 foot crane
to the top of a seven story building
we were to tear it down
but it tore up ahead of time.

I fell
like a dead weight
dropped
by an awkward god

Into the Light.

    My family and friends heard about the accident on the TV news and rushed to the hospital. The doctors couldn't initially give me any pain medication due to the high risk of internal bleeding. I saw Peggy and my folks for a few seconds before going into the operating room. They performed a lamendectomy to take pressure off the spine and removed shards of fractured vertebrae from the spinal column. The doctors said there would be some permanent disability and paralysis, but they couldn't say how much.

    During the weeks after the operation I experienced an overwhelming amount of love and support from my family and friends. Being class president and a soccer player I had lots of friends and the people at Crawford Long were kind enough to tell me we'd set their all-time record for number of visitors. The waiting area outside my room became a kind of gathering place for my friends, classmates, and teammates. After a few weeks I was moved from Atlanta to the world famous Craig Rehabilitation Center in Denver Colorado. Before the move, high on the morphine they gave me for the unremitting pain, I was forced to make a final decision concerning Peggy and Wendy. Only one of them could eventually go to Denver and help me through the rehab process. It was final decision time and I choose Peggy, the longer relationship. For better or for worse that was my decision and there's no sense questioning that choice in retrospect. So in a dreary hospital room, buzzed out of my gourd on an opium derivative, I said good-bye to Wendy.

All they being said, the really important aspect of the accident was my conscious experience of the process of death. Before describing my near death experience, I should mention that although I was far from being an enthusiastic Christian, before and during the 150 ft. ride up on the crane's pan, I said the Lord's Prayer, twice. The boss had handpicked a small crew to do the obviously dangerous prep work. The structure served as a large warehouse on the ground level with a mechanical building on the next level and three normal office floors on top, equaling seven residential stories in height. We got off on the top story and began undertaking the final preparation for its demolition, cutting what remained of the building in half. I was in front clearing the exposed rebar with a sledgehammer while behind me Lawrence and Donald were using a cutting torch to cut the rebar while Larry supervised. After a few minutes the building started shaking. I was swinging a large sledge hammer knocking concrete chunks off the rebar and didn't feel the initial vibration as the building began to shake. Larry reached out and jerked me around as he and my co-workers ran past me to the crane's boom and jumped on. It began swinging away from the building as I threw my sledge hammer down and began running towards it. I had to do what in track and field is called a running broad jump through the air to reach the bottom of the crane boom as it continued swinging away. Adrenaline fueled, jumping for my life I leaped out well over ten feet and caught the very bottom of the crane boom and felt my boss Larry reach out and grab me and help pull me towards safety. For a second we all thought we were going to be okay. Then there was a huge boom as the building collapsed out at the third floor and broke the crane boom like a toothpick. We fell to our seeming imminent deaths.

Next time you are riding a glass elevator look down from the 7th floor and calculate your survival rate free falling. The only reason we survived was we fell on mud and rubble, which was inestimably better than the asphalt nearby.

I was conscious the whole time we fell. Aware of the situation I clearly thought that God, my Momma, Peggy, and all the people that loved me couldn't do anything about the fact that I was about to die, just like a squirrel in the road getting hit by a car. I was about to die.

There was the sensation of falling rapidly, the air rushing up around us, the sound of men screaming and then whoosh! I hit the ground. But there was a distinct dual sensation at that point, my body stopped violently, seeming to jerk up like when a parachute opens, but my consciousness continued moving down into an ocean of white light. When my body hit it felt like diving into a lake, except the lake was an ocean of white light. A peaceful ocean of white light where love is palpable, all around you. My consciousness, me, I was a point of light in an ocean of light.

I remained a point of light in the ocean of white light/love a pretty long time. I stayed in this ocean of white light: while the massive dust cloud settled, while the police, fire, and ambulances arrived, while the others and I were located and my breathing passage cleared, while they loaded and transported me to the hospital, and while they prepped me for surgery. It was long enough for my parents to hear it on the news and for them to drive in from the suburbs to downtown Atlanta, park the car, and find me.

I popped back into my pain racked body right before they rolled me into the operating room. I begged a doctor to stop the pain and saw Peggy and my folks for a second before they wheeled me in. My body was not happy.
I do not know if I ever completely died by medical standards, I don't know about heartbeat and breathing; it was a co-worker, a descendant of pilgrim Miles Standish, who found me in the dust cloud and removed debris from my mouth so that unobstructed respiration was possible.

I consider this experience as do many who have experienced any of the now well known varieties of near death experiences, to be a real blessing, to know that consciousness exists independently of the physical body, and that Death is a Mystery we pass through initially into a spiritual world of Light. Once in Denver I was pulled off pain killers (except for weak-ass Darvon) and introduced to what a few of therapists called the "marine corps philosophy of rehabilitation". Instead of "Semper Fi" the attitude was "endure, aspire, achieve." We were to work ceaselessly to get back as much function as possible. As long as you could turn your head and move, you were to work hard and also to try to help your fellow patients. There was no sympathy, just the will to survive, adapt, get back as much function as possible, and continue on with life.

While in a Stryker frame, locked in the same position for two months, being flipped over every two hours, I wrote a poem titled "Strength".

Strength

Enduring is overcoming
Pain is an enemy
without a personality
just a force
that same force
we want to hit
our whole lives
but can't land a solid blow.

But yet enduring
enduring is overcoming
overcoming is winning
so man accepts
what happens to him
and fights
when and how he can
and endures.

For his own strength
is the weakness of his enemy
and the needed victory
for his soul.

Part II 1973-1974

For months I went through the strenuous rehab process. The final prognosis was that there would be permanent dysfunction and disability; paraplegia ranging between T-12 and L-1. My normal sensation and function level went down well below my waist on the right to the top of my thigh, but was higher on the left and in the back. I was completely healthy to the waist, had a grey area between my waist and mid-thighs, and had little movement other than spasms of the right foot from below the mid-thigh area. In the grey area, between the healthy and fully paralyzed areas there would be some sensation and some pain. In those areas, the nerve stimulus that came through were experienced as either pleasure or pain, hot or cold, wet or dry. Any irritation was experienced as an almost electric shock of pain. It was as though the injury had caused parts of my nervous system, at least temporarily, to turn upon itself and generate chronic severe pain

Throughout the rehab process, as I started going back out in the world, I developed a new awareness of how inept large segments of the generally well meaning public are when dealing with disabled people.

Don't Want Sympathy - Picnic in Hell

I don't want sympathy
neither do all the rest
of my disabled brothers and sisters.

There is no need for sympathy
that a car, or a bullet, or any other
of our society's implements of self-destruction
found someone their victim
for it could well be anyone.

Have not sympathy, but respect
for they have kept their sanity
held on to their dignity
and they kept their heads raised high
as they march through their own personal hell
day after day
a hell others cannot possibly comprehend
but yet they carry on.

Sympathy is useless
and brings on resentment
Respect and help, when asked for
can be used and appreciated by anyone
on a picnic in hell.

Although it was a difficult and agonizing time, I learned much from the accident and rehab experience and received a soul strengthening amount of love and support from my family and friends. This outpouring of love helped to restore an appreciation for the natural goodness and dignity of the human spirit.

Unfortunately, one thing that amazed me was the often offensive and obnoxious behavior of seemingly well-meaning people in relation to the disabled. I'm not talking about obviously rude behavior like staring and gawking, generally that comes from the uneducated and uncultured. My point is that people should simply learn to think before they speak. Who would go up to an extremely deformed, or obese, or mentally slow person and say I'm sorry that you have a miserable and pathetic life because you're ugly, fat, or stupid. Who would presume to get so insultingly personal with a total stranger or make such presumptuous judgments about a life they know nothing of. Well for some reason every (self-deluded) well-meaning obnoxious idiot in the world wants to come up to a disabled stranger and tell them how sorry they are for the pathetic, miserable, and pitiable state that person now finds him or herself in. Then nine times out of ten they want to relate some experience they've had or something about someone they know that they think is of interest or relevance. <u>It never is.</u>

The general public needs to be educated to treat the disabled as they would anyone else, and to offer assistance when and only if it seems absolutely necessary due to obvious physical limitations. Otherwise, treat the disabled with the same courtesy they do the AB (able-bodied). No more, no less. Effusive or persistent offers of help are obnoxious and unwanted.

After my rehabilitation was completed in Denver, Peggy and I returned to Atlanta. We went to a pretty decent local community college in the state university system; I got my life going again. My previous coach asked me would I join him as co-coach, but everyone knew he was the head coach and I was the assistant.

It is common with survivors of a widespread or personal catastrophe, that the experience begins or renews the survivor's search for the meaning of life, for truth, for the Source of All, for God, and the underlying purposes of existence and human experience. I studied the philosophical basis of the martial arts, concentration, meditation, and hypnosis with Master Jack Johns (Karate, Judo, Ju-Jitsu) who ran the Atlanta Black Belt Academy. Peggy and I would check out whatever interesting religious or spiritual experiences were open to us both within and outside of the academic setting.

For a while, after being invited by a classmate, we were the only white people to attend a black "holiness" church in southwest Atlanta. We read and studied a wide variety of religious and spiritual material in conjunction with our college courses on world religions, or whatever caught our attention.

A friend of my oldest brother whom I'd known and liked in high school invited us to come to a prayer meeting of "charismatic Christians." It was held in the offices of a real estate company and was obviously non-denominational and most of the people seemed genuinely sincere. I had been reading the Bible, among many other spiritual books, and had personally reached a point of <u>desperation</u> for some experience of spiritual realities. I wanted to know, to feel, to experience something real, not to just read or hear about such things. I wanted to experience something in the order of my near death experience; I wanted to perceive the source of reality. My near death experience had opened to me the reality, the power, and the certainty of personally experiencing spiritual realities. I wanted more. From personal experience I knew that what was written in a book; whether it was the Bible or some other sacred text, could not compare to direct experience.

These charismatic, non-denominational Christians believed in the reality of the Holy Spirit as described in the New Testament. They believed in healing, speaking in tongues, the interpretation of tongues and all the other gifts of the Holy Spirit. My knowledge and understanding of the wide variety of phenomenon produced by hypnosis and other techniques made me skeptical of what I saw in such charismatic circles, but I didn't doubt the sincerity of the majority of the participants.

At this meeting in the real estate office, praying with these charismatic Christians, I personally reached that specific point of desperation where I was willing to do whatever it took to know God, to experience Divinity. I prayed toward Divinity with sincerity and commitment. I just wanted to know my Creator and have some glimpse as to the why of creation in general, and me in specific.

I underwent an experience that I knew little of at the time, but was later to find descriptions of in various mystic traditions throughout history, an experience of a sudden transcendence, of a mystical Oneness, and of a spiritual Light. In reality, most cultures now and across time have had mystics who have reported and described such events. I eventually learned that such experiences were the central goal and primary theme of the Neo-Platonic philosophy, a philosophy believed by some to have exerted a profound effect on the development of both Christianity and Islam.

I only know what I felt, saw, experienced. It was well into the prayer service with individuals scattered around the room, some in small groups, praying silently or out loud. Some were speaking in tongues. There was an intensity, and a kind of spiritual ecstasy seemingly genuinely experienced by some of the participants. At this point I was praying silently, internally, just asking God to let me know He was there; saying I was willing to do anything to know, to experience something of Divinity, when my inner perception changed.

My eyes were closed, I was praying intensely, breathing deeply, when I began to perceive a brilliant white Light. It was a spiritual white Light expanding from a center, whose brightness of Light was past description. My perception of this Light, my experience of it seemed to be centered in my forehead, and with each breath I took in, I experienced a dual perception of both moving outward closer towards the center of the Light and at the same time I was moving deeper inside as well. I was not thinking in words, only experiencing, as with each breath I, my center, my consciousness, seemed to extend from my body's forehead going forward deeper and deeper into the Light; while at the same time the dual sensation that I was moving inside. Without words I felt a certainty, an intuitive knowing that I was perceiving something of the Spiritual Source, of Divinity, and that Its' essence was a combination of Power, Love, and Being. As this experience continued, with each breath I seemed to move closer and closer to the source and center of the Light. At a certain point, as I approached the very center and source of this spiritual Light, I experienced the clear and profound thought that I was not pure enough to go any further. As to the origin of this thought, it was not from me, not from my ego, my personal consciousness. I only know that I went no further into the Light, and gradually with each breath withdrew, eventually returning to my normal self.

Because I experienced this event with these charismatic Christians, Peggy and I continued attending their meetings for a while. They didn't ask for money, they didn't put a lot of pressure on us, so we kept going. However, the experience, nor anything similar was repeated. I also felt that while some of these people were genuine some were not, they were putting on a performance to go along, to be part. Faking it at church didn't cut it for me, it was very disconcerting. I did put forth the effort to read the Bible, cover to cover, and then reread the New Testament. I continued to search for a spiritual home that intuitively felt right, but could not find one.

However, I had 'the point of light in an ocean of white Light" near death experience and the "Divine White Light oneness/godhead" experience as my personal spiritual foundations. I now knew there was more to being human than being a bio-mechanism with five senses whose existence was the result of some cosmic accident without meaning or purpose as some scientists claim. Much more. The following poems dealing with Jesus and the religion of Christianity come from this period of time. The first of these poems was inspired by an experience I had in the seventh grade. In the spring of `66 a very straight looking science teacher read Ferlinghetti to his classes. Eight years later Ferlinghetti's images rose from my subconscious mind.

Christ Keeps Climbing Down

Christ keeps climbing down
in my mind
and reminds me of the things
that I have seen
and pushed aside

Christ keeps climbing down
in my mind
and reminds me when I bullshit
or plays around
with silly rhymes

Christ keeps climbing down
in my mind
and rebukes me for this criticism
I give voice to
all the time

Christ keeps climbing down
in my mind
and reveals that all this pain I feel
is not his
but just of life

Christ keeps climbing down
in my mind
to tell me I'm a child of God
as is all
humankind

Christ keeps climbing down
in my life
to rebuke me for my lazy weakness
and feed me strength
when I do right

Christ keeps climbing down
in my mind
to remind me of humanity's crucifixion
which leads me
to the Light

Christ keeps climbing down
in my mind
and tells me to get off this cross
and with joy
to rejoin life

Christ keeps climbing down

in my mind

and tells me everyone

is a child of God

and a God of Love provides

Christ keeps climbing down

in my mind

and releases me from the dreaded darkness

of his three days

in the ground

Christ keeps climbing down

in my mind

and whispers that his Father's Love

gave birth to Life

and all mankind

Christ keeps climbing down

in my mind

and remind me that there's more to life

than meets

the common eye

Christ keeps climbing down

in my mind

and reminds me of the bravery

of the life he lived

and sacrificed

for humankind

Christ keeps climbing down

in my mind

and then he climbs back up

for lost humanity

that we will not

be left behind.

The following poems also came from this period of contemplation on the life of Jesus, the man who came to be called the Christ, and my personal search for a relevant and intuitively acceptable Christianity. One built on Jesus' life, words, actions; a truly Christian Christianity. We couldn't find one.

One Inside

I knew He must be there
so I went looking
down the lonely streets and empty alleys
He seemed allusive

I met some people - claimed they knew Him
so for awhile I journeyed with them
I stayed to see what they would tell

and then I met Him, met Him with them
and I drank the water of that well
but I never felt at home there,
never felt at home within

I thought they knew Him like I knew Him
but still, I felt so far from home
as time went on I grew in knowledge
that deep inside, for me, they're wrong

they know Him only through their blinders
with their preconceptions they partly saw
but they could not take in the wondrous glory
and the tolerant love He does bestow

good they were, and still remain
but far from them I am again
but close to Him I now arise
soon with Him I will reside
in my own home,
with Him beside.

They, I'm sure, will make it too
in their own way
with all their rules
they'll see Him as conceived to be
He doesn't care, He bends and shapes
Meets any who will run the race
away from all the camouflage
and to the place we all reside
the One of all
the One inside.

Held His Own

He walked upon a sea of water
Held His own up on a cross
He healed the lepers in His presence
He sent the thieves out from his house

I wish we had Him here this moment
For all instead of just for some
To scare these modern scribes and Pharisees
Again most cruelly in control

Where did His pious way of life go
Is it in the cathedral's golden thrones
Or was it in the poor street life
and In the desert without a home

Jesus railed against the system
Blamed the evil on the richest
Drove the money changers outside
Took on Rome with spiritual might

We sure could use His strength again
To fight against these false pretenders
Who misuse his name and gather riches
Who claim to be good while doing evil

Jesus' Lady

Jesus looked at the young woman
He had tasted her sweet lips
and He loved her with a passion
that only young men can possess
But He knew He couldn't marry
it would chain Him to her side
So He left her for the Mysteries
she was not meant to be His bride.

But He thought of her sporadically
throughout the studious years to come
As he learned the wisdom of the Ages
and grew in spirit till He was One.

He would think of her so gently
and would smile and think of them
all the walks and warm embraces
and just how much she had loved Him
and He wondered who she'd married
wondered if she'd had a child
and he wondered if He'd see her
before his fated chosen time.

And He wasn't disappointed

when she came to hear Him speak
She was pleased, and she was proud of Him
as she sat there at His feet
and they knew that things were different
they both knew how it must be
and He knew His life went rightly
as He brought her to her feet
He smiled and said a prayer for her
and sent her on her way
And He knew that she, like millions more,
would follow in His way.

And His joy in this, known long ago
had ended any sorrow
the Peace He brought the world to know
was His mission, and He loved it
He accepted pain and sacrifice
as payment for the knowledge
that He so freely shared with all
who would break their chains of sorrow.

He knew He'd chosen rightly
since the day so long ago
when he left her love for humanity's sake
so that Love Itself would grow.

Little Things

No, I don't really worry about the devil
anywhere
except in the heart of man
I don't think God sits upstairs with a notebook
adding three fiery days for each "goddamn"
or four fiery days for drinking too much
or two for lusty thoughts
People should not worry about the little things
<u>just the devil in their hearts.</u>

I think the devil shows up
wherever there's child abuse
anywhere where humans are cruel
anywhere where there is hate

But I also think that God shows up
in our hearts and in our lives
if we try to do those things we can
to love and help all humankind

I think that life will be good and fine
when all the hellfire preachers have to do
is whine and complain about the little things
that we as humans are apt to do.

Part III 1974-1975

The next poem from this period reflects my growing awareness of the historical circumstances of the life of Jesus and the religion(s) that followed. My ambivalence toward certain aspects of Christianity continued, despite or because of my inner experiences. From early childhood I've always had an appreciation of Nature and spent much time in what could be termed a meditative contemplation of Nature's beauty. During my childhood I often spent hours lying on the grass on a small hill, watching the clouds float over. In fact, most of my early youth was spent playing in the woods, or in some other kind of intimate contact with Nature. I've always felt similar to the way Bob Marley described himself - a natural mystic. I've always felt that the Earth is humanity's beautiful and loving Mother, in a very real and actual way. This feeling is not reflected in the religions of "the Book" - Jews, Christians, or Moslems. Possibly this is because the Semitic people were desert people and faced a harsh environment or because the male and patriarchal hierarchies of the religious institutions feared any female aspect of divinity. Maybe if the biblical stories had come from a people living in a less harsh environment Nature would have received more beneficent treatment. A bible setting of Hawaiian or Native American origin would probably have been much kinder to the sacred feminine aspect of nature.

During 1974 Peggy and I met Ruth Stillman, whom I consider an American Saint. (Not a saint in the Catholic sense, but a truly saintly person. More correctly, she was a holy woman or Adept.) Through Ruth Stillman we became acquainted with the literature of the Theosophical Society, and a wide variety of other metaphysical and occult literature. The Theosophical Society was established during the late 1800's and early 1900's by a collection of bizarre and noteworthy mystics and occultists.

Because of the near illiterate and sensationalist quality of the modern media, it is necessary to define the word occult. Repeatedly. Occult simply means that which deals with the unseen aspects of life and a knowledge of the supernatural. It has nothing more to do with Satanism or evil than it does Christianity and good. By definition, all religions have an occult aspect in that they deal with unseen causes.

The Theosophical Society has an extensive library to which we had access. Through their literature and a wide variety of reading material I became aware that all religions have esoteric and exoteric dimensions. There is always a difference between what the general public is taught (exoteric-outer) and the knowledge the sacred practitioners are initiated into (esoteric-inner). I did some reading exploring the esoteric or hidden side of the Christian Mysteries and became more comfortable with the explanations of esoteric Christianity than those presented to me during childhood.

My personal explanation of this, most simply put, is that the Word, the Christos, the Love of God, the Christ Light, the energetic love of Divinity is approachable by humanity. It is a part or aspect of Nature, a naturally occurring dimension or level of consciousness. During some near death experiences, and sometimes during trance, meditation, or prayer people perceive varying degrees of this divine white Light/Love.

Each of us has a divine spark and we all come from the same sacred source or Godhead. By identifying with and experiencing a mystical union with our Divine Spark/Higher Self we also experience a communion with the Divine

Source. An enlightened person is one who had experienced this union and accepts that a spark of divinity is at her/his core, and at the core of all people and things, and attempts to identify with and come into harmony with this inner spark of divinity. The enlightened take a divine spark and become a spiritual flame. This experience of a oneness with all life and the divinity within leads people to varying degrees of enlightenment, expansion of consciousness, communion with the Higher Self, or transcendence.

In relating this to the life of Jesus as presented in the Bible one must look at the story of Jesus' baptism by John the Baptist. At the moment of Jesus' baptism when the Holy Spirit descended upon Jesus as a dove, his conscious mind experienced his own divine spark/High Self as well as a oneness and identification with the Divine Source or Godhead. At one with his Higher Self, he experienced the Love of God, the Christ Light, Universal Consciousness, the Holy Spirit. Thus did Jesus the man become Jesus, the Christed One, who has access to the Kingdom of Heaven within. The oral mystical tradition holds that from that moment Jesus' aura extended for a radius of two miles and people could be helped or healed by coming within that proximity.

He lived through the three years of his ministry in this state as a Christed One, in communion with his High Self and Godhead; with the Christ Light, the Holy Spirit, the white Light/Love of God flowing through him as an inexhaustible power. For the sacrifice at the end to be complete and perfect, Jesus the conscious man had to go through it without help. The union between Jesus the conscious man and his Higher Self, the kingdom within, the Holy Spirit, was temporarily lost during his crucifixion, as is stated by Jesus himself, when he screams out, "my God, my God, why has Thou forsaken me?"

By this explanation, God's Love, His Grace, the Holy Spirit, the Christ Light is a universal, omnipresent aspect of nature that any individual can access. It is waiting within, as the divine spark, the Higher Self. Although this is certainly not obvious in the outer physical world of reality, divinity lays waiting at the core of all created things. This Love of God is an aspect of Life/Existence/Reality available to all of humanity if they do what Jesus did by understanding that God is Love and the entire Kingdom of Heaven is within. Contrary to the standard exoteric Christian position, this union may be possible irrespective of the religion followed and the symbols used. In fact, the word yoga means union and we find this concept of a union with the Higher Self/divine in many cultures. I believe and was later taught that a God of Love would not turn his back on one of His created. Not a God of Love.

From its very beginning of modern psychology, in the works of Freud, Jung, etc., man consists of a id, an ego, and a superego, or a subconscious, a conscious, and a superconscious. I prefer the more simple low, middle, and High Self. In all of these systems the "me" of an individual is the conscious mind. The body, instincts, memory comprise the id, subconscious, or lower self. All these systems posit that man has a higher aspect, the source of conscience, morality, and spiritual experiences. This Higher Self is the aspect of human existence where man experiences the divine spark of divinity or in esoteric Christian terms becomes filled with the Holy Spirit, the Christ Light. If one accepts the reality of a Creator, of a God of Love, and then powerfully and profoundly experiences that reality in mystic union they will return to normal consciousness and relate that divine reality is beyond the scope of the human conscious mind, beyond rational explanation or descriptions, beyond limitations, and way past man-made religions. Once experienced, one accepts that this Divine Reality transcends all human limitations.

Remember that Jesus the Christ taught that there were many mansions in His Father's Kingdom. However metaphorically or actually one takes these words, it would be my contention that at least in one of these mansions this theology is surely prevalent.

Exoteric Exclusion

The sad thing to me
about the exoteric Christian position
is that it is competitive
You either make it
or you don't

You make the best - Heaven
or hit the worst - hell
and so you either win or lose
instead of everyone being involved
in this one great human experience
you have them
and you have you

an ideology that leads to a philosophy

of separation.

Everything

that grossly wrong interpretation

and lack of understanding

brings about

is contrary to the world view

of a God of Love

a God of Laws

A God of Spiritual Growth and Evolution.

During these years of intense reading and studying a few authors were strong influences who made lasting impressions. It seemed at the time that some books were read by almost everyone of my generation. Several who come readily to mind are Robert Heinlen's *Stranger in a Strange Land*, Aldous Huxley's *The Doors of Perception*, and Herman Hesse's *Sidhartha* and *Stephenwolf.*

In the works of Carl Jung I found a clear explanation of the concept of archetypes. Through reading Huxley and others I noticed that the various "ancient wisdom" traditions around the world, what Huxley called the "perennial philosophy" and modern esoteric Christianity had much in common and were surprisingly similar and harmonious in theology and philosophy.

Peggy and I took courses at Georgia State University in parapsychology by psychic, teacher, and author Evelyn Monahan *(Put Your Psychic Powers to Work , The Miracle of Metaphysical Healing).*

The wonderful thing about her classes was their experiential approach. I was once more surprised to find a great similarity, as anthropologist say, across space and time, between the various mystic traditions and psychic practices of cultures all over this planet. I also found interesting the concept of balance found in Chinese philosophy and mysticism - the Yin and the Yang in eternal balance, transcended and unified by the Chi - the Life-force. I was greatly impressed by the ancient Taoist text *The Tao de Ching*. I also found fascinating Hesse's descriptions of Abraxas - a God of good and evil, a God embracing the paradoxes of Life and Creation.

The next few poems from this period reflect my interest in Jungian archetypes, in the apparent paradoxes inherent in Life, and in the experience of spiritual realities, especially the white Light of transcendence which I had experienced and is so often described by mystics the world over. A recurring theme in these works is that of taking personal responsibility for one's life conditions and for one's personal growth and spiritual evolution.

Through my exposure to Theosophical literature I was acquainted with the Hindu and Buddhist concept of Karma. This concept has its parallel in the natural world, as Newton described in his laws of motion: for every action, there is an equal and opposite reaction. Jesus taught that as you sow, so shall you reap. In anthropology we learn that one of the few cultural norms in every human culture is the law of reciprocity. When reciprocity breaks down, so does the stability of the culture. The whole problem with concepts such as karma is that people start wondering why did this specific event happen? The "why me" syndrome. These questions, I think are problematical.

Concepts like the golden rule: do unto others as you would have them do unto you, are wisdom worth guiding your life by. But wondering too much about the past causes of current events can be more of a distraction than an aid. Ruth Stillman shared with me two thoughts that are relevant to these questions of karma/cause and effect. The first is that the <u>intention</u> behind an action may be more important than the action itself. The second is that it is not so much what happens in your personal world, but how you <u>react</u> to what happens that is important. Evelyn Monahan said the same thing quoting an old axiom that relates to the ancient but often dubious practice of astrology, "a wise man rules his stars, a fool lives by them." Ruth, who fully believed in the law of karma, expressed to me her opinion that one's karmic debts are fully paid when an event happens in the physical world. The individual is free to react however he will to that occurrence. But of course, those new actions accrue new and future karma, which will be either positive or negative, depending on one's intentions and actions.

Write Our Character

We have accepted many Archetypes
and live by them
we intuitively feel our Higher Nature
until we experience our Higher Being
and then live through the Paradox
it always brings.

When we have written our character
according to how we use the Archetypes
and then we discover
our <u>Real</u> <u>Self</u>
and then the War begins.

And we totter back and forth
and live on the Edge
until we have the Best
of Both Worlds
and then Transcend them.

Paradox

We are all Paradoxes

by our constitution

We are doomed one

till we grow past the Lower

And absorb the Higher

but until then

The Animal

The Learned

And the God

Within us conflict

And war for domination

of the Consciousness

Each trying to influence

Each grasping for Control

We live

And breathe

And Love

By Paradox.

Self-Responsibility

It may be that the only thing
you have to take "on faith"
is your own existence.

For through the experience of your existence
you can feel "God"
if you want to bad enough
transcend time and Life's chains
if you want to bad enough
and even live through dying
if you've tried hard enough.
Once you take your own existence
as a reality
and take Responsibility
for yourself
It's all left up to you
just what you do with it.

Blaming it on luck and fate and all
the other excuses
Never really satisfies the Self.
And those that use them
Are never satisfied
deep down inside.

Moral Evolution

The more we learn of ourselves
the more our responsibility deepens
We've heard for a long time
to love thy neighbor as thyself
But explicit instructions
are hard to come by.
We have to trust our hearts
and they often make mistakes
by which we grow
"positive reinforcement of Negative
Actions and attitudes by loving
Acceptance leading to dysfunction"
is all very complicated
but probably true.
What we knew 2000 years ago
has to move on
with what we learn today.
Man is evolving morally
as well as mentally
and must take advantage
of all his growth.

Inconsistent

It seems we find as humans beings

that few things

Are all encompassing

We find ourselves inconsistent, but tend to think

others do not share our faults

But when we look close enough we find

all is inconsistent

All the attributes of man are not one sided

or overwhelming

We may be afraid of no living man

but scared of rats

We may be very mature in business

but at home - childlike

Few things, except our choices, seem consistent

we can grow or not grow, as we choose

We can stay where we are, or go backward or forward

it's up to us to choose.

We aren't wise enough to understand

everything going on around us

We're not always smart enough to even

monitor ourselves

But overall, we have a choice

and no one can make it for us.

The choice is ours.
To choose and live by.

Seen the Light

Perhaps there is more order
than I'll ever know
Perhaps I'm just a robot
in some damn big ten cent store
Perhaps our whole damn Universe
is but a single atom
in the cell of some poor worker ant
in a living room terrarium.

If it is, or if it's not
I doubt I'll know real soon
But I have felt the One
I've seen the Light
And once for me's enough
to Know we're not alone
to know at least
in some small way
there has to be a Plan
and the Light I felt

Was Pure, was Love
and Pointed toward the way
that I could find the freedom
to grow in my right way.

Know I Don't Know

Maybe when one reaches
by crushing his selfish self
God Consciousness
he will need no loving
or maybe he will be truly free
to practice free love.
I do not know
I've only been there once
and know enough to say nothing
about something I can not explain.

The White, the Light

the Beautiful White Light
may be the Source
or it's reflection
may be the Whole
or my reflection
I only know
that I don't know.

But in seeking God
by crushing my selfish self
the ego self, the separate self
I may find
that I know more of God
than I now think
or maybe I can feel God
instead of think God.
I do not know yet
I only know
that I don't know.
And I want to know more.

The Only Creature

We waste so much time

it is unbelievable

so much of the time

we spend our Life

with the attitude

that what we do is boring

How can we be haughty

about something we can't understand

Who of us knows

the Why

of Life

or how our consciousness

has come about

So much time flies by

never appreciated

for the wonderful

and mysterious thing

Life is.

We human beings

in all of Nature

in all of <u>Our Reality</u>

we are the only creatures
With Self-Awareness
and a separate I
with past and present
and a bio-computer
and most important
<u>an imagination</u>

We are so special and unique
until we reach
by growth
into the Higher Reality
where we can see
we are but children
But until then
we're at the top
of this reality
Most leaders of humanity
must have had this realization
of the great importance
of Living Time.

And the scale of this reality
in comparison to others
would lead a person

to understand his place
and to appreciate this Living Time
enough to learn to use it
and to learn more of Life's wisdom
and to use that precious knowledge
to help and lead the others
who have not yet reached the glory
that awaits them deep inside.

Edge of the Known

He said he too
sometimes almost goes over
the edge of the known world of reason
over into the other world
which seems like magic
because it deals with why's
instead of how's
because it's filled with causes
instead of reasons

the edge is scary
and one must steady oneself to stay
it takes courage and fulfills the archetype

that proves one's bravery

we are all descended warriors

and we must know about the warrior life

in order to grow past it

and the warrior life is fighting

not only outer evil but that within

battling within oneself

to know, to learn, to grow

and to remain within that other world

that shows this world's illusions.

And facing yourself in that reality

it is not easy

Being masters of the lower

we must cooperate with each other

Being servants of the Higher

we must take our place at the bottom

and grow again.

Another blessing that results from a near death experience, besides the certainty of something more, something spiritual and good beyond this life, is a great appreciation for life. Once you accept the certainty of your own imminent death, but escape it's jaws, you feel a profound appreciation for that life.

Everyone should look up at the stars on a clear night, and think of the magnitude of the Universe, and then realize that this beautiful little blue planet Earth is the only place in the cosmos with conscious Life as we humans know it (at least so far, and definitely in our area of the Universe.) How unique and wonderful Mother Earth is to be the womb of life, especially human Life. In our little part of space/time we are it. Jesus told us how unique and wonderful we humans are when he said "know ye not that ye are already as the gods themselves." I never have heard a minister give a sermon on that aspect of Jesus' teachings. The theme of the following poem is that conscious existence is such a rare and exquisite gift, it deserves vibrant celebration.

Vibrant Celebration

New Year's Eve - one more year gone by
from childhood to adulthood
I know the loss
but sometimes fail to see the gain.

It's a time for celebration
but when I think of time passing

of childhood joys gone by
and never to be had again
in quite the same way
I feel a sadness
the sorrow of a childhood lost
innocence never to be felt again
the awareness of right and wrong
sometimes binding the natural feelings
of an Abraxas child.

I feel the sorrow
but I also feel the warmness of the Light
the Light of heightened awareness
of growing understanding and love
for what I see and those I know.

It is a time for celebration
to hide the sorrow of a forever lost past
and to praise the wonder
of a forever distant future
and to celebrate the truest
wonder of all
that we exist in the now
and existence being the greatest gift of all
Deserves a vibrant celebration.

Of course, from `72 to `75 there was more going on than just my spiritual search. Peggy and I were living together with my brother Winslow and our Vietnam vet cousin Emmel in the downstairs of a huge Victorian house in Decatur, know by the fame of its previous owner as "Hanging Judge Hardy's house". I continued my daily battle for better health and function despite the severe chronic nerve pain. It is not that the pain was ever present, it wasn't. However, not an hour would pass without a pain spasm or two. It was not constant unless I had a bladder infection or fever. Then it was every six seconds, like a knife thrusting in with 50,.000 volts running through. Getting to sleep was always difficult. Effective medication for pain or sleep was still decades away at this point.

Peggy and I continued our less than passionate relationship. We were going to college and life kept happening. At this time I was fortunate to be in a position to be on the founding Board of Directors and participate in the beginning of what was to become a nationally respected rehabilitation hospital which is still performing a valuable service to this region of the country. My life was a paradox itself, in that in some ways things were really pretty good, but in other ways pretty lousy.

Beauty and the Beast

The sadness comes damn near
to overcoming me sometimes
Late in the morning
watching the ugly TV
with its' ugly commercials -
looking in the mirror
and seeing quite a paradox
half health, half death
both improving, I hope
but still - Beauty and the Beast

I'm a lot like the world
part of it whole
part of it not
some of it alive
some of it dead
it's the Beauty and the Beast, too

The whole damn thing
comes close to overcoming me
around 3 or 4 AM, till I
get to sleep
or sit down and regroup my energies

and feel the pulse
of my insurmountable inner strength.

I'm a child of God
made in his image
Our strength I think
may be relative
to how much we know that
whether cognizantly
or intuitively
of course that
like all statements
is probably part true
part untrue
Beauty and the Beast, again.

But when I think
that each of us
if we only took the time
to look deep inside and find
what we need to make it
and be happy
we might find it waiting there for us

the true Beauty

in what can be

and sometimes is

the Beast.

My brother Winslow inspired the next poem. He was quite the ladies man at the time; he had *it*, good mojo, sex appeal. He sometimes worked in bars as a doorman/bouncer, and other times just hung out. Whatever, he spent a lot of time successfully pursuing joyous, if less than meaningful, unions with the members of the opposite sex.

To the Young Man Spending all his Time Chasing Physical Gratification

I might say to you how you waste

your time

and how you really can get too much

of a good thing

But what's the use

you play your games

I play mine

while most of those around

are playing business, greed, or power games

or other games

much worse to me
than all your love games.

After all, if you're going to get
stuck in a rut
Sex ain't a bad way to go.

Some poems are just passing comments on Life, or what was going on with my family and friends.

Communication

It would be much better
if we communicated in emotions
and didn't have to fool
with these bunglesome words.

People mean entirely different things
while using the same words
both taking for granted
that the other understands.

Words get in the way and lie
feelings seldom lie
but seldom get expressed.

It's too bad we know no way
just to share our feelings
instead of sharing words.

    I came from a big family with five kids. Growing up our father was strong and quiet, our mother outspoken and commanding. Dad pretty much let Mom run the show until something really important came up that he felt required him. I had a brother two years older, and one a year older, and a much younger brother and sister. We had a loud, often joyous, always active household. Like any big healthy family we played a lot, fought a lot, we always loved and sometimes hated, but all in all it was a wonderful and stable family base.

    I have been extremely fortunate to have the same best friend, Tom, since the summer of `67. Since we went to the same school, and along with his brothers and my brothers, we all played sports together, we became part of each other's extended families. His grandfather was one of our best soccer fans and was a fine example of an elegant, dignified, and able senior citizen. He was a true Christian, he lived it, although he seldom attended church. His church, like Tom's and mine was Mother Nature. The following two poems concern Mr. Watkins, known as Popper, when his lifelong wife passed away.

She Is Not Gone

She is not gone
she yet, is with you
though in body she abides not
she is in your heart

She is not here
but she is happy
she now knows more
of God and Love.

You'll miss her in your daily life
her absence is a constant sorrow
a loneliness which makes life harder
and she can't ease away your pain

But when you listen to your heart
it tells you softly
that she's alright
she's gone on to her spiritual home
in time with her you will rejoin.

But it the meantime life goes slowly
while the grief inside you builds
but yet, the Life inside you rises

never ending - overspills

Angrily you turn to God now
Questioning all the things you've seen
but down inside you know the answer
your heart reminds you
that this must be

But Life, you know, is never ending
she and you will meet again
patiently she's waiting, loving
and once again with her you'll share.

The sorrow now is yours alone
No one else can know your grief
Her presence lost cannot be lessened
God knows you'll miss her smiling face.

But time will help you overcome this
Love and Peace are yours to share
being is a worthy challenge
a glorious duty, a mighty task.

Your head is raised, your courage rises
embracing Life, you earn our praise

as always your life shows the beauty
that the Peace within you brings.

Life is flowing, always forward
she's just ahead of you, upstream
know this river is always moving
towards the Ocean of God's Peace.

She said I Love You

She said "I love You"
and she meant it
at a time of great loss
the simple and the true
was all that could be said
so she said "I love You."

She was not his daughter
or even close family
not even a relative
but an employee
someone who
in the confines of an office
had grown to love and respect

one so deserving.

At this moment of greatest sorrow
the most painful loss in all his life
He epitomized strength, and grace, and honor
despite the fact his wife was gone

He stood there stoically
accepting the tragedy
which would have brought
other men to their knees
instead of indulging in his own sorrow
he consoled others and eased their grief

the weight of the world
burdened his shoulders
while the dignity of Mankind
shown in his face
she could only kiss him
and tell him she loved him
it was all she could do
and all she could say.

During this time a cousin of mine, a beautiful young girl, was taken prematurely by cancer.

Susan Is Gone

I hardly knew her
except that I prayed and hoped for her
often during this year

She is dead, She is gone
No force on this Earth
can bring her back
the sadness her family feels
is one felt long and hard
the kind of pain
that can change one's outlook
on everything

If I didn't believe that Susan is somewhere
in a spiritual state
I don't understand
if I wasn't sure
that Life's everlasting
I'd have broke down and cried

when I heard the news

Instead I just hid, hid my emotions
hid my emotions and kept watching TV
and prayed to God that she was in Heaven
and didn't feel cheated
by a life incomplete

Let her not feel the loss
that's felt by her family
and let them not grow too bitter
at Life's tragic ways
and though none of us know exactly
what follows Life's passing
grant us a certainty inside
that her spirit's at Peace.

Another of my high school friends was involved in her own spiritual search. She was later to work for the Campus Crusade for Christ. Who knows where our spiritual quests will lead. Mine was to lead me to a Northern Paiute Sweatlodge; hers was to the work of Billy Graham and then on to missionary work in Russia. So it goes.

Starts her Searching

Donna quits her life and starts her searching
seeking for something to give her
peace of mind
the security she needs, a few questions answered
and she just wants to know
if God is there.

And if you want to see Him
do they keep Him in the churches
and let you have a glimpse of Him
on Sundays once a week
or is He with the people
as they live by all their rules,
all the little rules
that help them feel secure.

Donna keeps on looking here and there
looking one place, then another
trying to find her self
or some answers she can call Truth
or <u>the Truth</u>, if she gets uppity.

She'd like an unplugged lamp
she wants to get the electricity

and she's trying all the sockets
to see which one has the juice.

She may just learn
hopefully very soon
that it's a wonderful lamp, indeed
which plugs into itself.

My relationship with Peggy continued and in some ways evolved. She, like Tom and I, and so many of our friends loved the beauty of Mother Earth as was well expressed by our generation spearheading the environmental and ecological movements of the time.

Peggy and I were very close, we had shared so much in both good and bad times, and we seemed to be on the same spiritual quest and journey; but things were far from perfect. We were different in personality, she was shy and reserved, while I was more confident and outgoing.

I was a Nature-lover, but also a people person, or at least I found people fascinating. She, at the time, was not much of a people person at all. We had been teenage sweethearts, but we had grown up quickly after my fall, going through the rehab process, and then starting over. We were close, and shared a strong love, but it was no longer the romantic or passionate relationship it had been before the accident. Our love existed, perhaps in some ways even stronger and deeper, but she had a lot of trouble adjusting to my damaged body. She fell in love with an athlete, but ended up with a man savaged and damaged by life a few years later. It was not easy for us.

Different

A long time ago

I chose a little girl

and she chose a young boy

and we began.

Different then and different now

to others it seemed strange

that two so unalike

should grow so close

and be so harmonious.

She is unique in my eyes

quiet and unaffected

with a controlled ego

only dominant when needed.

She is loyal, she stands by me

though I am undeserving

she is loving in her own way

as I in mine.

We don't get along perfectly

but we mostly get along

and we change and grow together
while so many grow apart.

Two So Young

I pride myself in her
but seldom show it
I feel my love swell inside
but little does she know it
except for how I live
and how we stay together
through much more
than two so young should have to.

She has been my example
of constant strength
She has been my example
of grace and beauty
She has been my teacher
and been my pupil
as I've been hers

But most of all she's mine
not in owning but in loving

and she has me the same
and as we grow together
towards Peace
we'll keep searching in love's name.

Middle Aged Doldrums

Sometimes, when I look at us
I think the middle aged doldrums
have set in prematurely
and sometimes we both wonder
if we really love each other.

But then I see you smile at me
or feel your love for me
and my only worry
is that you feel my love.

When I see myself be childish
or act foolish
and watch how you put up with me
I am amazed.

I am a brat sometimes

like some spoiled little child
and you scold me like a mother
or I catch that look you make
that tells me I'm being obnoxious
and brings back the natural me.

As one flit once said
our love is not a blazing fire
but unknown to her
.or any of her shallowness
our love is deep and lasting.

We are the yin and the yang
two opposites - which compliment
and form a whole.

A whole which sees the both of us
transcend our roles
unconsciously and naturally
a whole that lets us be ourselves
our worst and best
when loud or quiet
when happy or sad
and lets us be a whole
whose foundation is love.

Although on the surface, and on a spiritual level, we got along fine and were very close, there was still something lacking in both our lives.

Alone

Love windes on an empty mind
Like snakes
drawn in the sand

And love calls
the ape in all
to get on with the Plan

And love beckons
the little boy
to build one more sand castle

And I call
to a Princess far
to come on to her prince, now

And love calls
and the silence falls
and I'm alone, again.

The next few poems are just short political and social comments about the times, `73 to `75.

Today's Children

I think the main difference
between yesterday's children
and today's
is not that today's children
have all the answers
it is that today's children
know today's parents
don't have all the answers
and aren't expecting them
anytime soon.

Society, which provides all the tools
for a firm foundation of disillusionment
has the impudence to act surprised
when that disillusionment becomes apparent
it did not catch on, it's not a fad
it's a product of the times
and of the people who make the times.

It's a natural result of education
showing examples of logic and common sense
while society shows so little logic
and almost no common sense.

Nixon & Company

Bullshit, Bullshit, Bullshit
coming down all around
very little but lies from high places
and lies describing high places
and lies passing for history
and lies passing for news.

Very little is really said
that I have ever heard or felt
that really got down to the truth,
that all but a small minority
are motivated purely by self-interest,
even the most devout, even the wino.
One likes to feel secure and chosen,
assured of everlasting life
the other likes not to think
and drinks his way to bittersweet escape.

Which is more honest?
I do not know
but the wino's path is at least direct
which has to count for something.

With my previous coach, Scotty O'Neil, I had returned to soccer and was coaching some players I had previously played with. Scottie was a successful amateur coach and was later a successful collegiate coach, and at the time we had an under-18 amateur team that won the state and southeast championships and went on to San Diego to play for the national title. One night we went across the border to Tijuana. It was my first real experience in a third world economy sleazy border town.

Tijuana Blues

I wonder whether I'm scared
to not look at tomorrow
as business as usual
or to take a look tonight
back over my vacation
to find out what I learned
about the world, about myself.

My big question about vacations
is it seems to raise the issue
when people go on a vacation
is the vacation to or from a place
or a vacation from themselves
is it a vacation from society
all its' rules and moralities
a vacation from their daily life
and all the games by which its' played.

I saw the brazen ladies
in that brazen Mexican border town
the cesspool of the United States
just a fence away.
It made me think about many things
about the Mexican hookers
once you realize that your vacation
is their job, they never leave.

They'll be prostitutes tomorrow
when the soldiers and the sailors
go back to the loving wife and kids
or to be a deacon down the street.

Church or brothel, which is more honest?

      which institutions does the most good
      which heals the most
      or eases the most pain
      who knows, they both may serve the needs
      of their clients, and each other.

    I grew up hearing I was of Scott, Irish, Scott-Irish, English, Cherokee, and Creek descent. As I began my spiritual search I was interested in learning about the spiritual traditions of my ancestors. I read about the religious, magical, ritual, and mystical traditions of my European forbearers, and read what I could find about Cherokee and other Indian nation's beliefs and practices. Some relevant books were at the college library, but at the metaphysical bookstores I found, among other works, books about the Cherokee medicine man Rolling Thunder and Lakota visionary Black Elk. I read about the Sweatlodge and the Sacred Pipe. The large numbers of similarities of beliefs and attitudes between the pre-Christian western Europeans and the Native Americans immediately caught my attention. Especially the concept that the Earth is our spiritual as well as physical Mother.

    Whenever I heard the phrase "Mother Earth" as a child I intuitively felt an inherent rightness about it. Growing up, bit by bit, I had learned about the respectful and loving relationship that Indians have with the Mother Earth and all the creatures who live upon her. I've always had a great respect for that tradition. When I first heard the Catholic phrase "the Mother of God" it was like a bell rang. What had always been missing in the patriarchal, Mid-eastern based, protestant Christianity was finally realized. Humanity may well have a spiritual Father, Godhead, and Creator, but humanity just as surely has a spiritual Mother who physically bears us and sustains us.

The Indian's respect for the Mother Earth was apparent in every aspect of their life before European contact. It is unfortunate that European diseases and military might performed wholesale genocide on America's indigenous peoples. The western world would have greatly benefited and been decades further ahead in environmental sanity if the military conquerors of this continent had adopted its native inhabitant's respect for Mother Earth. In developing an industrialized America, respect for natural beauty and an aesthetically high quality of life took a definite back seat to whatever was quick, easy, and profitable. The following poems reflect my respect for American Indians and my love for Mother Earth.

Strong and Brave

Oh Indian, stand strong and brave
let not the white man hurt and rape
a culture he should emulate
Resist, take not the white man's ways
a society built on Nature's rape
a culture hated by your face
or should be with the days gone by
and wars that wiped out many tribes

and robbed your way of life from Earth.
You fought the white man in your ways
you fought and fought to no avail
you were overwhelmed by a culture stronger
in the ways of war and war machinery.

Now the fight continues to save your culture
if you don't resist then you will suffer
the loss of more than just your past
you're part of the Earth, and you must last
fight every way in which you can
to get things done, win back your land
let not the white man hurt and rape
a culture he should emulate
lay down the peace pipe, put on war paint
Oh Indian, stand strong and brave.

Dominion?

All our lands may not yet be
married to the lord of industry
but though it's not been won
its been molested
our virgin areas are no longer virgin

they've been raped by saws and dozers
pulling, ripping, tearing, killing
destroying Nature's precious balance
bringing sorrow to our Mother
For the Earth, and Earth's Life are one.
Although we set ourselves apart
say we're masterful - say we're smart
where's the machine that's mastered Nature
that can stop an earthquake
silence thunder, or prevent a flood
No, there's never been a one.

Nothing in man's meager mind
can equal the beauty of Nature's Might
and all that we pretend to know
are meager gifts She does bestow
deluded mankind has not dominion
deluded mankind has not dominion.

Nature's Children

Well, my friend
we're just two poets looking for eternity
two children looking for a place to play
two men looking for their women
throwing away the rules
refusing all the games to play.

We are followers of Pan
three thousand years too late
we're the children born of Nature
but we've somehow been misplaced.

This time and place we're living
is enough to make us cry
So we fight, but know we're losing
but we know that we must try.

Mother Nature calls out to her children
to come to her defense
enough's enough for anyone
even Mother Earth.

Well, we've grown through many troubles

seen the changes that have been
and our friendship just grows stronger
cause we know that we are kin.

We must live for Mother Nature
be her ally, fight her fight
or forsake our own true natures
fight our love and fight our right.

Yes, we'll stay together brother
through all the things to come
for the battles are soon to be raging
and we know that we can't run.

We will fight for our great Mother
for there's no way to repay
all the peace that she has shown us
in the beauty of her way.

Overwhelmed

I'm not ashamed to marvel at Nature
it doesn't embarrass me to enjoy a flying kite
or to spend my time watching wind play through the trees
or to stare at stars on a cool and moonlit night

The mountains and the oceans overwhelm me
I am awestruck and made little
by their magnitude and might

Mother nature is my mother
and my father is the Sky
I was raised on land and bathed in sea
and have flown throughout the skies

I'm a child of my dear Mother
and have little use for man
for his buildings and contraptions
that clutter up her lands

I know that I can't change them
or make them disappear
their followers are more than we
and addicted to their plans

that put our Mother second
and glorifies little man
or at least his concrete images
he has raised throughout these lands

But my mind is hers
and hers alone
I'll not change the way I am
I only hope that lost humanity
will re-discover Nature's plan.

God Gave

God gave man such beauty
man gave God such ugliness
God gave man Nature in perfect balance
and man destroyed that balance
God created weather
man tried to subdue it
God gave man water with fish
man gave God sewage and pollution
which poisoned his water
and killed his fish
God gave man the sky

man gave God air pollution
from countless cars and factories
in ceaseless motion and commotion
God gave man trees and forests
and man gave God cities
full of man's polluting toys
God gave man the Earth
and man gave God concrete
to cover the earth and kill the plants
and suffocate the soil
God gave man countless wonderful animals
man let God watch as he killed them off
some now gone, some soon to follow

God gave man a wonderful mind
which man wasted while dwelling in the material
God gave man variety
and man gave God contempt and prejudice
God gave man neighbors in faraway lands
man gave God war and unlimited destruction
God gave man a beautiful act of sharing
man debased it, and sold it
ignored the spiritual aspect and spoiled it
or played it like a game
God gave Life to man

     and man showed God

     a way he could destroy it

     God gave everything to man

    and man showed thoughtless greed to God

    God cried as He watched wasteful man

   mankind just laughed while he self-destructed.

  Carl Jung coined the term synchronicity, to describe what takes place when two seemingly unrelated events occur in relation to each other. Ancient humanity universally believed in signs and omens. Freud believed there were no accidents, but rather that human events were unconsciously propelled. The Chinese believe we are interacting with an evolving primordial Life force which was responsible for creation and is ongoing and evolving. In my own interaction with Life I began to see that Life could be perceived as expressing itself through a living symbolism. Or possibly, that everything in Life could be looked at, perceived, or understood through symbolic terms. To the American Indians, the circle is a very primary symbol.

  Eve Eaton used to show me how almost every aspect of life could be understood through the symbolism of the circle.

  In Christian symbology, winter equals death, and spring equals resurrection, the re-birth of Life. Long before Christianity existed, the shortest day of the year, the winter solstice (Dec.22) was considered the symbolic death of the sun, always accompanied by rituals of rebirth and then followed by the springtime. When Christianity was adopted by the Roman empire and was forcibly spread through Europe, the church placed Christian holidays on top of the pre-existing holidays. Throughout Europe the shortest day of the year, December 22, was the symbolic death of the sun. By the third day it is obvious that the days are getting longer, thus the sun is reborn. Jesus was given a December 25th birthday; superceding the previous dying sun gods he was replacing.

Spring

The resurrection is Now
All the Life
is off the cross
and bathing in its springtime beauty
before our eyes.

Human words and human thoughts
are useless at describing
they can only bring back pictures
to the minds of those who hear
for the pictures tell the story
of the colors, of the glory
of the so-much-more-than-man-could-do
that happens in a day

And it's there for all to see it

and it's there for all who'll live it

they can have that essence in them

and have it all the time

it's the Death of Death in Life

it's the ending of the strife

that Mother Nature shows to us

when her body comes to Life

There are no words deemed worthy

to describe the God-like beauty

of the blooming of one flower

when the Resurrection comes.

Many of the Christian mystics and esoteric Christians who believe in reincarnation and the evolution of the human soul also consider the life of Jesus to be symbolic of the path that all souls should, and eventually must take. Just as the years have their cycles of summer, fall, winter, spring - in an endless cycle of rebirth, they believe that each soul must eventually go through a similar process as that exhibited in the life of Jesus. They believe each human must experience the death and crucifixion of the selfish me-centered ego to have a resurrection of identification with the Higher Self, the divine spark within, the Kingdom of heaven within, the larger I, the Superconscious. But of course, for most people this process is not expected to happen at once, but gradually over many lifetimes.

When spiritual people in various cultures around the world start throwing around the words eternity and infinity many of them are much more comfortable with a series of hundreds or thousands of lives during which the soul accumulates wisdom and evolves than a one life, 75 years, then heaven or hell for eternity scenario. Not much room for mistakes in the latter without a theology of forgiveness, so thank Jesus, we have one.

For those esoteric Christians around the world who believe in reincarnation, as do the majority of people on this planet, this process of the evolution of the human soul and spirit takes place over a long, long series of lives. The western world view embracing the "one life - heaven or hell for eternity" scenario, besides being a minority position on the blue-green planet, does not seem as logical or as well ordered as the reincarnation hypothesis. My near death experience, white Light experience, and other later mystical experiences have not been personally informing concerning the process of the evolution of the human soul and spirit. For all we know there may be more than one simple mechanism at work in the evolution of the human soul. For those conservative Christians who wonder how other Christians can believe in reincarnation, they need only to reread their Bibles. According to biblical prophecy the messiah could not appear on Earth until the prophet Elijah had returned. When asked about this Jesus responded the Elijah had returned and was not recognized, referring to John the Baptist. If John the Baptist was Elijah <u>then this is an example of reincarnation</u> plain and simple.

Another example of reincarnation in the Bible is shown during one of Jesus' healing miracles. His disciples asked Jesus why the man born with a birth defect had been so stricken, was it due to his parent's sins or his own. Jesus did not refute the idea that the man could have accumulated sins and punishment before his birth in the present incarnation, rather he side stepped the issue by saying the man was born crippled to show the power of God, and at that point Jesus miraculously healed him.

For God to use reincarnation to return Elijah, means that Christians must accept that reincarnation occurs, at least on special occasions. The mystic and esoteric Christians who believe in reincarnation think we all go through a process of many lives, eventually through our own personal crucifixions and eventually experience our resurrection as a Christed spirit, at one with our Higher Self, the Divine within.

In my personal life, it seems I have followed a path filled with lesser crucifixions and resurrections. Don't we all.

Crucifixions and Resurrections

I believe that everyone has their own unique path, and in a way, must find their own unique truth. My life has followed a pattern of ups and downs, crucifixions and resurrections, swings of the pendulum, the balancing of extremes. However one expresses it, we all experience these rhythms, just as we have all had the odd occurrence, dream, or event in our lives which seemed personally important and upon which we later pondered.

Every kid has highs and lows. I came from a warm and loving family with an excellent educational base. But when I started school, I was a skinny kid who had suffered from bronchial asthma, had a few allergies, and spoke with a slight speech impediment. Yet I went on to have perfect attendance the first nine years of school.

By the time I was in the 5th grade I was playing halfback and middle linebacker in football and could speak clearly without effort. Then we moved, which is always hard on kids. By the second year at my new school things were great again, but by then it was high school time, time to start over again at the bottom.

Tired of losing fights to my older and larger brothers, and tired of being skinny, I began to work out and train as a boxer. I grew in statue and got to the point where I could defend myself against my older and larger brothers or pretty much anybody. By my senior year I had grown from being a skinny kid to president of the senior class and captain of the soccer team. I had accomplished all the goals I set for myself in high school. Within half a year I went from a kid on top of the world to being busted and broken in half. This seeming pattern of ups and downs throughout my life was not to stop with the rise and fall of a teenager, but continued.

All in all, I would say that I had an idyllic childhood, and up until the summer of `72 had a pretty wonderful life. The pattern of crucifixions and resurrections in my life had been mild up to that point. However, this pattern has caused me to look back over my life and ponder some odd occurrences that seemed to foreshadow or symbolically emphasize this pattern of crucifixions and resurrections.

One such incident happened during a time of play and fun as a child. My brothers and some neighborhood kids were playing on top of an old grape arbor that had blackberry bushes and other vines growing up all around it. We were yelling, screaming, throwing stuff, having good clean kid fun when I unknowingly stepped off the wire framed top of the arbor and fell off into the thorn bushes. All the kids stopped playing as I screamed in agony.

I was caught by the thorns of thick blackberry bushes around my legs, my arms, my head, and my feet couldn't touch the ground. I was suspended by the thorns cutting into my body under my arms, and I was not a happy camper. The first comment made, even before my brothers started yelling for my mother and then running to get her, was that I looked just like Jesus. Indeed, I was caught in the classical crucifixion position, with my arms straight out, one leg straight down, the other slightly bent. There was even a branch of thorns like a crown around my head. I was in pain, encouraging those running to get help quickly, while everybody else just stood in front of me telling me how I looked just like Jesus. My mother came and cut me down with a machete while my brothers tried to support some of my weight. When I was finally cut down, which took some time, I was scratched and bleeding, but the wounds were superficial and healed quickly.

The next strange and seemingly symbolic event took place many years later, ironically, the day I was baptized. Contrary to the practice of many protestant faiths where children are baptized at birth, the Baptist tradition is baptism by conscious choice. I have already gone into my reservations concerning the faith I was raised in, and I made the choice to be baptized along with my brother Winslow a few years later than most of the kids at church. But I finally did accept the Christian faith and joined the church.

A few hours before I was to be immersed in the large baptismal pool behind the church's altar, I was pierced by a nail. We were playing in the woods behind our house in an underground fort that was pretty much just a hole in the ground with a piece of plywood on top. As I slipped under the plywood to get in the fort, an unseen bent 16 penny nail in the plywood pierced the skin on my left temple and ran in for what seemed like an inch or more alongside my skull. I was less than thrilled at my predicament and used the full range of my somewhat ample vocabulary to express my displeasure. As one kid crawled out to go get help, he accidentally shifted the plywood which luckily pulled the nail out instead of pushing it deeper in. I had already had my tetanus shot, so two hours later I was baptized.

What Jung or Freud would make of such events I do not know. But I'm sure I would like Jung's explanation better.

I've already mentioned how, at the moment I was falling the seven stories, I mentally compared the inevitability of my immediate death to that of a squirrel being hit by a car, an extremely common phenomenon in Atlanta. While driving in Decatur one afternoon, during the time of these last few poems, I was directly in front of Agnes Scott College when another of these seemingly symbolic events occurred. I saw a squirrel running across the road on a collision course with the car in front of me. The squirrel hit the car's rear wheel and was thrown about seven feet straight up in the air. At the top of its flight, as it started to fall, I identified with that squirrel. For whatever reason, I thought about my own thoughts as I fell, how I had accepted my immediate death, just like a squirrel getting hit by a car. Obviously this squirrel is history. Miraculously, I watched the squirrel fall down the seven feet, land on its feet in front of my car, and although obviously shocked and shaken, finish its journey across the street.

Silly as it may seem, but because I had instantaneously identified with the squirrel, I took this as synchronisity; its miraculous survival strengthened my hope that one day, I too, would recover fully.

I don't know what to make of such events. I only know that they happened, and as I look back at my life, so far, I see a recurrent pattern of crucifixions and resurrections. I see that pattern in Nature and throughout all Life. Whether you say crucifixion and resurrection, the balance of yin and yang, an upward spiral of a swinging pendulum, however...Life continues through its processes of birth, life, death, and rebirth. It is the pattern of Life, the way of Life, or as the Chinese say, the Tao, the Way.

Part IV 1976-1979

Peggy and I continued our search for knowledge, our spiritual quest, together. We moved to west Georgia so Peggy could attend West Georgia College. I had collected many books and been given half of a personal library by an esoteric Christian, Liberal Catholic Church priest Father Brian Brinkerhoff; who had moved to California. I didn't enroll in the university but rather chose to read and study the material I was interested in and to daily roam the woods behind our rented house in extended communion with Nature. Although there was companionship, friendship, loyalty, and love, Peggy and I were farther away than ever from our passionate and romantic beginning. We both felt enriched by each other but we also had conflicts and were emotionally unfulfilled. I figured my life was tough enough and made more difficult by chronic pain for which there was no cure or remedy short of constant medication, so I felt it was okay to drink and party some. I was given an infinite prescription for Darvon. It was not strong enough to deaden the pain, but anything available at that time that would be strong enough to kill the pain would have been in the opiate family and addictive. I threw the Darvon prescription away.

I have mentioned that I was more of a social animal than Peggy, my love of partying, music, and nightlife was something Peggy didn't share. Her mother had been a hard drinker throughout her childhood and the experience had left her with little interest in drinking/partying/merrymaking. As time continued our relationship became more strained.

I moved to Augusta for the spring and summer of `76 while Peggy stayed at West Georgia. My brother Winslow, and my best friend Tom, and I tried to reclaim an old abandoned family home that had fallen into an abysmal state of disrepair. We fixed it up somewhat and lived rough, but we couldn't come up with the funds to put in a new well, water pump, and plumbing. While in Augusta visiting friends much of our stuff got ripped off which soured our enthusiasm. At summer's end Tom went back to college, Winslow and I moved back to Atlanta and Peggy took off with friends on a trip out west.

I have a long history of driving very safely when I have passengers in the car, but too fast when I don't. I've out grown it now, and learned my lessons, but it took me way too long. Anyway, I launched a `72 Olds Toronado (with a 454 cubic inch engine, 4bbl. carb, rated at 400 horsepower) into a hundred year old oak tree at high speed. I almost lost my left eye, I broke my right leg, and both ankles. Peggy came back and when I got out of the hospital Winslow, Peggy, and I got an apartment.

At this point our loved and respected teacher Ruth Stillman told me that a friend of hers, a writer, a healer, and a part Native American shaman was coming to Georgia and she could arrange a meeting if I was interested. I certainly was.

Eve Eaton, author of over twenty books, respected shaman, and the woman I call the Grandmother of Métis Shamanism, came to write a book at an artist's community up in the mountains. Although I didn't know it at the time, I later found out that Ruth and Eve were two of the thirteen highest level initiates in the world in an offshoot order of Freemasonry. Called Co-Freemasonry, it is a world-wide order in which the men and women work their initiatory rituals together, contrary to normal Masonic practice in which the sexes are segregated.

Eve, as was Ruth, was in her early seventies at the time. Eve had written a variety of books, among her most famous was one about Lincoln, *Quietly my Captain Waits*, and a couple of them had been made into movies. She wrote three books about her fight with cancer, her healing, and her initiation into shamanism : *The Snowy Earth Comes Gliding, I Send a Voice, and The Shaman and the Medicine Wheel.*

Winslow, his girlfriend Fay, Peggy and I went to visit Eve a couple of times at the artist community. She practiced the spiritual healing techniques she had learned from Paiute, Arapaho, and other Indian medicine men and healers. She burned sage, used eagle feathers and a round healing stone, she smoked a sacred pipe and she prayed.

The Sacred Pipe Ceremony is equivalent to the Christian Eucharist and Holy Unction. When an Indian smokes a sacred pipe the whole universe is ritually put inside the pipe. The individual communes with all of creation. It is a beautiful and moving ceremony.

I showed Eve things I had been collecting for years: feathers I had gathered from hawks killed road-side, a deerskin taken from a fawn road-kill, and a small smooth stone Evelyn Monahan had given to me which she had brought back from her trip to the Great Pyramid in Egypt. Eve showed me how medicine men and women used feathers and rocks as spiritual symbols and tools of spiritual healing. Then she invited me to come visit her at her home in California, where I could study with her, meet her teacher and possibly attend his Sweatlodge. For someone of part Indian heritage who was interested and eager to learn more about his ancestor's ways, this was a dream come true. So much happened so quickly over the next few years I can only hit the highlights. I won a lawsuit against those responsible for the demolition accident/injury and for the first time I had the freedom to go and do as I chose. I made three extended trips to California to study with Eve and was accepted into the Northern Paiute Sweatlodge she attended. I went through the extensive and intense four day ritual used for a major healing or becoming a shaman.

Peggy and I continued moving further apart, but we still felt bound to each other. I bought an old log cabin in the North Carolina mountains. It was without running water or electric power and needed much work. The terrain was so rough and the conditions so primitive I kept an apartment in Atlanta. We drifted farther apart but we had so much time and emotion invested in each other we couldn't or didn't have enough sense to let go.

So Peggy, by choice, lived in the cabin. I bought her a car, a truck, and the horse she wanted. She and some of my friends, who lived there off and on, were improving the cabin while I visited often but lived in Atlanta. As our relationship became more distant and strained we decided to try an open relationship. I told her I would provide for her if she would respect and honor three requests. I asked that as she developed other relationships and made love to other people would she not do that at the cabin, to let that be for us. I asked her not to date anyone in our circle of mutual friends, or anyone that I employed. In return I agreed not to date any of our mutual friends or to take anyone else to the cabin.

Of course, you cannot put restrictions on the human heart and Peggy feel in love with one of our friends, who worked for me fixing up the cabin. Unfortunately, the two of them lied to me and the rest of our mutual friends about their activities for an extended period of time, more than a year.

When the truth finally came out, it was the prolonged deception that hurt those lied to. I had chosen to believe her over what some of my friends had hinted at and what my intuition told me. Being deceived for so long while I paid the bills upset me tremendously and at times made me quite irrational. I went through a long dark period, listening to Linda Rhonstadt and Jackson Brown sing their saddest and most depressing material, during the daytime, with the shades pulled down, drinking heavily. I bought a .22 magnum revolver and put the word out through our mutual friends that if my ex-friend, ex-employee Kenny came to Atlanta, I would not hesitate to do him bodily harm.

It was a very bleak period but with the passage of time and a little help from my friends I got over it. With the help, among others of Lisa, Laura, Nancy, Rhiannon, and Meagan, over a period of several years, I got over it. During these relationships with the aforementioned women, for periods ranging from between three to nine months, or longer, I rediscovered romance and passion. What a wonderful rediscovery it was.

Peggy eventually went out west and studied with Eve. She later studied acupuncture, was a chiropractor and holistic healer, now does deep tissue work. She married a chiropractor/artist and they had a son, got divorced but still live in close proximity. She runs a clinic in California. I wish her well and as the years passed the animosity faded. At the time it happened I hadn't made many of the mistakes to which I would later succumb. I was young, to some extent inexperienced in the ways of the world, and very possibly somewhat self-righteous.

At the time of the revelation of the extended deceit there was a final separation; she left the cabin, kept the car and the truck, left me to deal with the horse, and went west. I felt anger and outrage.

Damn Deceiver

I don't want to make you guilty
I don't want to make you sad
I never will quit loving you
I just don't want you around
I was giving you good loving
At least I thought I was
At least I told the truth to you
You kept saying that you were
Well woman of so many years
You are gone now from my heart
You know it's not damnation
I just want a brand new start
A few months without thinking
Of the lies and the deceit
The fool that I was made of
It was clearly there for me to see
I didn't want the truth then

> Now truth is my desire
> and I finally have my freedom
> But the price I paid was high
> Oh, damn deceiver
> How could you lie to me
> You who taught me honesty
> now have taught me dark deceit.

The reader must remember these years represent that period of time after the sexual revolution but before AIDS. I would say that, in general, I practiced serial monogamy. I would get involved in a romance, we would let it go as far as seemed natural; maybe three months, maybe six or nine, and then move on. I wrote many love poems over a two or three year period and finally experienced a wider variety of partners. I learned much about women, about human nature, and about love. And I had <u>fun</u>.

Lisa was my first new love after so long a time of being emotionally unfulfilled. She was a waitress at a country-rock bar, what she called a good confederate bar. We had a whirlwind romance. She was an artist who drew fairies, mythological figures, and work with an occult theme.

Lisa was a black haired beauty, with long luxurious wavy hair, who was quite the femme fatale. She never lacked male attention, and was not big on loyalty or fidelity. She had the option to go with me to California, but in the end backed out to remain in the night life where she was comfortable.

Although our romance ended when I left, our friendship and affection did not, and she became a roommate at my house on North Druid Hills Road by `78. The following poems are about Lisa and my rediscovery of romance.

Sweet Smiling Woman

Sweet smiling woman
I want you to know
how soft, warm, and tender
your love is up close
the weight of the future
on your shoulders, unknown
relax and just let the light
in your soul shine forth
Kriya I name thee
the sweet grace of God
that you should be here now
as my friend and my love.

We Could Be

Woman sweet woman
you're wise and you're quick
your eyes can see deeply
and you're not taking shit
we could be lovers
and we could be friends
or we could be over
before we begin
I've been too nice, or
been around way too much
I've shown you my ass
while I ran drunk amok
and you have been patient
while I've been morose
through the punishment I earned
with a failure so dark
so now I have started
starting over again
soon I'll be leaving
still, you keep me here
we could be lovers
and we could be friends
friends for a long time
if we both show some sense.

Ocean of Our Love

These eyes so overdue for tears
this body over-killed with scars
these eyes that looked so deeply back
that first time, down into your heart

And the Ocean sees and knows
and the Ocean tells no lies
and the Ocean has its own life
its own ways of wrong and right
and the Ocean is our growing love
and that Ocean is so deep
and that Ocean holds a strong peace
that may yet be ours to keep

In words known yet never spoken
understood though never heard
the pledge of love a binding
the full completion of our needs
the communion of the joyous ones
who have found and understood
reveals potential of an endless love
past our dreams and past mere words

In words known yet never spoken
understood though never heard
revealing now, Love's Ocean
Mysterious Vastness without end
this joyous peace so new to me
found only at your side
has brought the wondrous joy of Life
once more, clearly to my eyes.

Illusions Shattered

We have had our illusions shattered
we don't live out old ideals
we have seen our trust be crumbled
by the ones that we most trusted.

We must learn
Humility through silence
Power through Knowledge
Light from Life

As I bring order to my world
may I act in knowledge

that one day I will leave it

as I create in this world of illusion

make I walk on the exodus away from shortsighted industry

as we return to the Path of Righteousness

and the Way of Sacred Nature.

Dreams of Rings Shattered

My dreams of rings

and only ones

so long ago

were given up

so short a time

and they were shattered

This crazy life

it gives up slowly

to the ways of duty

to the ways of Light

surrenders all its secrets slowly

so slowly...one by one

the veils go by

until it does reveals its splendor

and gives you love, and gives you love

love sweet love
love sweet love.
This might not be
all illusion
just good sharing
which brings us through
this might not be all illusion
just real sharing
just real good
but who knows what will happen tomorrow
tomorrow your eyes, they may grow cold
but I am hoping
my sweet sister
that you will be my water brother
that we can bring each other joy
that we can be as lovers-friends
for we don't live in love's illusions
that held out love as a fantasy/dream
we know it comes and goes a lot
without changing faces, only names
but love brings tenderness to the evening
love brings the passions of the night
and I know the beauty of your body
in the early morning light
and I'm hoping that you're feeling

in your heart

like I in mine

such rough waves

from early on

we have met and we have swum

obstacles and threats have come

we have met them

we have won

from the struggles

from the passion

love and power we have regained

obstacles will come against us

and once repelled, will come again

in our present, darkness falls

but the light we have

is the Light of Love

we always feel it

we're always home

the Light we have

is the Light of Love.

Beauty at Sunrise

I wish that you could see as I
Your beauty as our Father rises

After loving through the night
to see your beauty in the light

Bright-eyed one with skin so soft
upon me let your dark hair fall

And as our love so freely pours
higher and higher in spirit soar

Until, when right, we then shall find
that moment of oneness - heart and mind.

Lisa and I had a fun relationship that was good for both of us and our friendship continued after the fling. As mentioned I had offered to take her with me to California, but she had chosen to stay in the nightlife, so I went on in search of wisdom and healing.

California - Laura and Chris

I met Chris and Laura one night on a stopover as I was coming back from the Sweatlodge, heading for San Jose and Eve's friend Doctor Gail, another healer of repute. I was on a natural high from my experiences but I was also ready to have some fun and socialize with some people of my age and subculture.

That first night when I met Chris and his sister Laura we became instant friends, a friendship which continued through the years. Chris was doing various jobs while trying to launch a music career and Laura was a recently divorced music teacher with a three year old boy who was more than a handful. Laura and I had an intense romance that was as spiritually fulfilling as it was passionate, and in many ways a healing experience for both of us. Our romance was cut short, however, when her previous romantic interest who had been on the way out had second thoughts and from out of nowhere proposed. Laura wanted and felt she needed a father for her child and a stable nuclear family. Having finally escaped the octopus-like hold of one long term relationship, I was not ready to accept any such responsibilities. I went back to Georgia for a while and when I returned, Laura was married but our friendship continued.

Chris played piano and guitar in his carport/studio and we wrote some songs together. We went into a professional studio and made a demo tape but I couldn't get my financial advisors in Atlanta interested. In 1979 I got involved in another project, and we put our musical collaboration on hold. Because I was working with Chris on music during my California visits, most of my poems during this period ended up being lyrics to songs for which Chris wrote the music. The following two poem/songs describe phases in my relationship with Laura.

All That I Wanted

I came here for work that's not easy at best
and with you on my mind there's so little rest
wrestling with demons is not easy or fun
this work's so important, but then so is our love

(the refrain):
All that I wanted was to have a good friend
but now all I want is to see you again
all that I wanted was to have a good friend
but now all I'm wanting is your love again

I've got to find out what we're going to do
about this sweet love that's so shiny and new
all that I want is to be in your arms
to find some true peace, and lay my head on your heart

All that I wanted was to have a good friend
but now all I want is to see you again

all that I wanted was to have a good friend
but now all I'm wanting is your love again

All that I wanted was to have a good friend
and damn if I didn't go falling again
but with you running off to see your other friend
it makes falling in love so hard again

All that I wanted was to have a good friend
but now all I want is to see you again
all that I wanted was to have a good friend
but now all I'm wanting is your love again

All that I want is for this love to work out
I'm wanting your love and to get back to work
All that I wanted was to have a good friend
I didn't bargain on falling again
All that I wanted was to have a good friend
now all I'm wanting is your love again

All that I wanted was to have a good friend
but now all I want is to see you again
all that I wanted was to have a good friend
but now all I'm wanting is your love again

All that I wanted was to have a good friend

I didn't bargain on falling again

I wish I didn't feel so good in your arms

so when you leave me alone it would not wound my heart.

It's a Damn Shame

Well I'm so damn tired of driving

but I've got to leave this town

my being here without you

is bound to bring me down

I'm heading for the desert

I need some good clean air

I want to see some stars above

cause I know that you're not there

(the refrain):

It's a damn shame

I don't like the way - I fee inside

I want something

that I understand - cannot be mine

I wish that I could find the words

for the way I feel inside

you're flying to another man
but I'd like to make you mine
I swore I'd never feel this way
but here it is again
I feel so strong this love for you
I want to be your man

It's a damn shame
I don't like the way - I fee inside
I want something
that I understand   -   cannot be mine

I know that it must bother you
of some things I won't talk
my jealousy is showing
but you won't hear it from my mouth
I wish that I could be your man
but only for a while
I love to share this happy life
and sleeping in your arms

I'd like to be your only man
for a couple of months at least
or maybe for a half a year
and then always be good friends

this love we share together
it seems so good and strong
but if I don't have my freedom
my warmest love grows cold

It's a damn shame
I don't like the way - I fee inside
I want something
that I understand -   cannot be mine

I'm not asking for I know ahead
your answer must be no
I want your love but then in time
I'd want my freedom so
At first we'd be so happy
then restless I'd become
we'd feel that it was slipping
then you'd turn to find me gone

It's a damn shame
I don't like the way - I fee inside
I want something
that I understand -   cannot be mine

I wish that you could understand

my conflict of desires
how I love to feel your softness
and to see your bright eyes shine
but I'm married now to freedom
I wear freedom's wedding ring
I know that freedom owns me
and this desire to stay would fade

I wish that I could help you know
the Goddess Earth I serve
My life to her I gladly gave
my freedom she returned
the Power that I draw from Her
is a light that fills my soul
Her love is there for all of us
who love and serve the Earth.

It's a damn shame
I don't like the way - I fee inside
I want something
that I understand   -   cannot be mine

Métis Shamanism and Sweatlodge Christianity

The following poem/songs were the product of my experiences and friendship with Eve Eaton and her teacher whom I refer to as Grandfather Raymond. Going through the four day Sweatlodge ceremony at Grandfather Raymond's Sweatlodge was one of the high points of my life as was the opportunity to live near and study with Eve.

I have made no effort to hide my ambivalence toward the religion I was exposed to during my childhood. I used to find the atmosphere during a church service stifling and boring and the sing-song delivery of a sermon almost always put me to sleep. I used to joke than instead of being a narcoleptic, someone suffering from a disease of spontaneously falling asleep, I was a churcholeptic, who went to sleep every time he went to church.
For those who are curious about the Sweatlodge ritual I suggest Black Elk's book *The Sacred Pipe* where he describes the Oglala rite of purification, Inipi. Although I went to a Sweatlodge run by a Northern Paiute, the description of the Lakota Sweatlodge is very similar and probably the most thorough available in print. A Sweatlodge is a small dome, shaped somewhat like an igloo, covered by hides or canvas, in which (usually) somewhere between ten and twenty people (there is no specific number) sit in a circle and sing sacred songs around a fire pit filled with rocks which have been smoldering in a fire all night. There are four rounds, the first is a call for help, the second and third are the working rounds for healing and prayer, the fourth round is for giving thanks and smoking the sacred pipe. It is a beautiful and moving ceremony.

One of the things that both surprised and pleased me was that Grandfather Raymond, Eve, and most of the other participants at the

Sweatlodge were Christians in their own way. I call this "Sweatlodge Christianity" and it can be found at various Sweatlodges all over this continent. I'm not saying that all Sweatlodges are peopled by Christians, they are not. There are still many traditional Indians way back on the interior of some reservations that consider Christianity nothing more than the religion of the invading conquerors. But in my experience, most of the Sweatlodges I know of personally, contain some members who practice Sweatlodge Christianity.
In the same way all religions have an exoteric and esoteric aspect, my study of world religions has taught me that religions are either inclusive or exclusive in their doctrine and practice. In some instances different sects within one religion may exhibit either characteristic.

    A right-wing, one-way Christian would be an extreme example of an exclusive attitude, as would be a radical Muslim cleric. Either <u>knows</u> that their truth is the <u>only</u> truth, their way the <u>only</u> way, their beliefs the <u>only</u> <u>true</u> beliefs, and that all others who don't believe as they do are <u>wrong</u>. And to the fanatical, literalists Christian, all others are doomed for eternity to a fiery hell. The exclusive religion, simply, excludes all other beliefs, doctrines, and views. They are right and everybody else is wrong.

    The inclusive religions, of which Sweatlodge Christianity is an example, is usually an indigenous faith which holds on to their original and traditional beliefs as a foundation, and then includes and absorbs those parts of other beliefs that come along which seem to work, ring true, or are felt to be perceptually verified by experience. Sweatlodge Christianity is being practiced quietly all over North America, both on and off the reservations. But it should be made clear that the Christian part is an addition to the pre-existing beliefs.

Sweatlodge Christianity is not organized, institutionalized, simply a way of describing those with traditional practices who have made a place for some Christian beliefs and symbolism.

In the Caribbean and parts of Central and South America, and now in the U.S., especially in Florida and Louisiana, original African beliefs, transplanted by slavery were mixed with Christian beliefs and practices producing such systems as the Santeria, Obeah, and other forms of Voodoo. Asia provides many examples where Hinduism or Buddhism, or both were mixed with pre-existing or indigenous belief systems.

In Sweatlodge Christianity, the indigenous shamanic system adds the new Christian elements to their pre-existing beliefs, spiritual hierarchies, and practices. Because the religion brought by the missionaries, and more recently by evangelicals and fundamentalist is exclusive, the shaman did not join them and give up their previous beliefs. But because the symbols and images of Christianity grew to become powerful and pervasive in their culture they were added to the pre-existing shamanic belief system.

When asked to explain this practice, a medicine man or woman may tell you that the Indians already had Jesus, before the Europeans showed up. Indeed, among many Indian nations there are myths and traditions of a teacher of righteousness whose mythic identity is similar to that of Jesus. At least one book, *He Walked the Americas*, by L. Taylor Hansen has explored this theme. However this belief is not central or fundamental to the mix of some aspects of Christianity with the pre-existing indigenous beliefs and practices. Instead of arch angels and angels the native American shaman has Grandfather spirits and animal or nature spirits. Where Christians have the

Word, the Creative Logos, the Indians have the Thunderbird Eagle/Thunderbird Man, from whom came the Grandfathers of the four directions.

In sweatlodges I have heard Jesus referred to as "the Star Child" because his coming was announced by a star. They accepted Jesus as a healing spirit of love. But there is no talk of eternal hell, no dependence on the Bible or veneration for its Middle Eastern origins, or its doctrines of exclusion (the saved - the elect, and the damned). The Star Child now exists besides Grandfather Eagle, Grandfather Buffalo, Grandfather Bear, and all the other Grandfather Spirits, but the Bible is considered a book brought by the Anglos and Spanish when they invaded. The stories and myths about a previous teacher made this inclusion occur naturally and easily. The Native American shaman continues to work with and experience the spiritual realities passed down to them continuously by their ancestors for an estimated 30,000 to possibly 100,000 years. For this they need no book. Nor do they want one. In the simplest terms possible, Eve explained to me that the Earth was our Mother, the Moon our Grandmother, the Sun our Father, the Sky our Grandfather. Every Star is an individual being, as is each animal and plant. Among the healing spirits is the Star Child, whom the Anglos call Jesus. All Life is interconnected, and all living beings are related. In fact, everything that exists is related to every other thing in the family of Life.

The Christian has the Logos, and the four Beings before the Throne, the angel, the lion, the eagle, and the bull. In astrology the angel is Aquarius, the lion is Leo, the eagle is Scorpio, and the bull is Taurus. The Indian has their own equivalent, the Thunderbird Eagle/Thunderbird Man from whose eyes come lightning and whose wings beat thunder, who gives rise to the Grandfathers of the four directions, the four powers, the four primordial elements (earth, air, fire, water).

At the Sweatlodge, for the first time in my life, I could be a Christian in a spiritual relationship <u>with</u> nature, not outside of it, or in (pretended) dominion over it. For a clearer and more detailed explanation of this the reader is referred to Eve Eaton's *the Snowy Earth Comes Gliding.* Or my own work, *Shaman Between Worlds.* Included here is a chart from my writings as an anthropology student when I returned to college in the early 1980's. What follows are poems/songs inspired by my exposure to the Sweatlodges and the teachings of Eve Eaton.

Grandfather Eagle

Come to me I pray Grandfather Eagle
come heal my body and my mind
I've avoided my Creator for so long
I'm finally ready for Thy Will to be mine

(Refrain):
All the children have to come to the White Light
the Kingdom of Heaven is buried inside
the way to freedom is by helping your brother
Love's the strongest weapon, let's turn the tide

Come flying I pray Grandfather Eagle
carry me to the realms of rose-love
lift me to the sphere of gold-wisdom
then lift me into the White Light

Come to me I pray Grandfather Eagle
help me from the anger I feel today
Man is killing the life of this planet
he poisons the water, food, and air while I sing

Come to me I pray Grandfather Eagle
explain to me why there's no peace today
help me to know why they rape my poor Mother
use me, I beg you, to help her today

Come flying I pray Grandfather Eagle
I know that their ways will soon end
but please leave the green Earth for your children
I swear we can have Eden again

(Refrain)
All the children have to come to the White Light
the Kingdom of Heaven is buried inside
the way to freedom is by helping your brother

Love's the strongest weapon, let's turn the tide

Come flying I pray Grandfather Eagle
I know that their ways will soon end
but please leave the green Earth for your children
I swear we can have Eden again
I swear we can have Eden again
I swear we can have Eden again.

Try to Justify

(Refrain):
I don't care what you say
to try to justify
I don't care what you do
there ain't no reason why
Take a look around you
don't you hurt inside
Look now at this planet
My God why don't you cry (alternative - try)

Look now at your children
they want to ask you why

they want their world to make sense
they want to know you tried

Look now at your children
they won't take all your shit
they're searching hard for freedom
hell bound now to find it

(refrain)
I don't care what you say
to try to justify
I don't care what you do
there ain't no reason why
Take a look around you
don't you hurt inside
Look now at this planet
My God why don't you cry (alternative - try)

Everything God put here
starting now to die
all your lame excuses
just look like bald faced lies

the food, the air, the water
soon it won't be fit

look at just how guilty
you really are of it

From South Africa to south Boston
by any name its hate
Capetown to Watts to East L.A.
what's wrong, it must be fixed

(refrain)
I don't care what you say
to try to justify
I don't care what you do
there ain't no reason why
Take a look around you
don't you hurt inside
Look now at this planet
My God why don't you cry (alternative - try)

Look now at your planet
look now at your greed
soon your goddamned money
will be all that's left that's green

You're wiping out the elephants
rhinoceros and whales

there's nothing that you get from them

you can't get from something else

(refrain)

I don't care what you say

to try to justify

I don't care what you do

there ain't no reason why

Take a look around you

don't you hurt inside

Look now at this planet

My God why don't you cry (alternative - try)

You're killing all these animals

till there won't be any left

I don't understand your ways at all

are you evil, is it hate

You don't think about your children

or the world you're going to leave

you don't care about you grandkids

all you care about is greed

(refrain)

I don't care what you say

to try to justify
I don't care what you do
there ain't no reason why
Take a look around you
don't you hurt inside
Look now at this planet
My God why don't you cry (alternative - try)

I don't want your factories
that you built so proud
don't want the nuclear technology
that you spread around

I don't care about the gold
that I know you made
I don't care about the growth
while you watched the Earth get raped

I don't think you care about
your children's life to come
I know that you don't care about
this Earth we all live on

I know that you don't want to hear
what I've got to say

but the way you've spoiled this planet
well it may have sealed our fate

I don't care what you say
to try to justify
I don't care what you do
there ain't no reason why
Take a look around you
don't you hurt inside
Look now at this planet
My God why don't you cry (alternative - try)

Why Have You Stopped It

(Refrain):
She is Isis, She is Quan Yin
She's the Virgin Mary and She's Aphrodite
She's been worshipped on this planet
since before recorded time
why have you stopped it
The Earth She is alive, She is our Goddess
Mother Earth She is alive, She is our goddess

The American Indians know Mother Earth,
as the Hindus do
the Wiccans praise Our Lady,
and the Taoist know her too
all religions of this planet Earth
know her by different names
she gives our very life to us
why don't we praise her name

(Refrain):
She is Isis, She is Quan Yin
She's the Virgin Mary and She's Aphrodite
She's been worshipped on this planet
since before recorded time
why have you stopped it
The Earth She is alive, She is our Goddess
Mother Earth She is alive, She is our goddess

The Mother Earth is calling out
to Her children far and near
too much damage being done to her
she warns that we must stop
we've got to help our Mother Earth
not deplete her till she's weak
we've got to take good care of her

She's the source of all we need.

(Refrain):
She is Isis, She is Quan Yin
She's the Virgin Mary and She's Aphrodite
She's been worshipped on this planet
since before recorded time
why have you stopped it
The Earth She is alive, She is our Goddess
Mother Earth She is alive, She is our goddess

In <u>Memories, Dreams, and Reflections</u> Carl Jung describes how we have little dreams that everyone has every night and are quickly forgotten. Then there are the rarely occurring great dreams, which one never forgets and has a lasting impact on one's life. It was during one of my return visits to Atlanta between my trips to California that I experienced such a great dream. I took an afternoon nap at my house on North Druid Hills Road in Atlanta and experienced a dream that made a lasting impression. At its conclusion a neighbor's Doberman began barking loudly, insistently, and I awakened with the dream fresh in my mind. With pen in hand I immediately recorded the details of the dream. The experience is described in the following poem, although using poetic license I substituted "night" for afternoon in the text.

Jesus in a Dream

I finally met the Lord of Love
it was in my dream last night
and the things He said to me
have opened up my eyes
I've never felt such love before
or seen such tolerance
there are many ways to Spirit's Heart
and mine is one He said
He didn't claim the only path
there are many more He said
He said that we were only One
He said that Love was all there is

Well I met Jesus
the Christ who is the Lord of Love
Well I met Jesus
and He taught me tolerance and Love

I finally met the Lord of Love
and beside Him saw the Light
I saw Him heal the battered child
I felt Him pouring Life
He wasn't quite like I'd been told

> He didn't claim it all
> He said He walked the way of Love
> and that all souls would come home
> He told me the Creator
> the Spirit who made Life
> had given Man free will to find
> the path back to His Light
> He said that everyone must choose
> the path of their own soul
> that in the mind of Our Great Spirit
> all religions art but one
>
> Well I met Jesus
> the Christ who is the Lord of Love
> Well I met Jesus
> and He taught me tolerance and Love.

Returning to a more mundane and emotional level, after loving and losing Laura, I returned back east. I met a nurse, a midwife in the mountains whom I'll call Meagan. She had been living with a man for years but was unhappy with her situation. She told me she was getting it together, preparing to leave him. In rural North Carolina, that's not as easy to do as it would be in a more urban setting, due to the lack of available housing and employment opportunities.

We had a romantic, passionate affair for a several months. Having lost Peggy to deceit and Laura to marriage, I was probably on the rebound, and badly in need of the ego-stroke of romantic love.

Wanted Gift

It hurts because it's something real
breaking down and changing
It hurts because she looked me in the eyes
so deeply
It hurts because it felt so good
when I was with her
It hurts because of so much time
spent smiling

But now I'm betting on these signs
and omens
I'm betting that I know my wants
and needs
I'm betting on a wanted gift
from Heaven
A gift of healing love
that sets me free

There is something reassuring
knowing
there was something about me
other
than my spiritual quest for knowledge
and true power

something warm and human
something manly
That such a sweet, kind, warm
and gentle
soft, strong, fair, and beautiful
woman could love.

Please Be With Me

You looked so alive and happy
when you went driving off
I had felt so alive and happy
until you said you had to go.

Please be with me.

You say you want to
but can't let go

Please be with me.

Oh shit
it's all so crazy
I told an affectionate friend
down in Atlanta
that I was only good for three months
she said she wanted nine
I told her she could have them
but that was long before you smiled.

Oh shit, it's all so crazy.

And you living with a man
who you say brings you down

It's All so crazy.

You the strongest lady
in so long an unknown time
You say you felt you'd held me
before our bodies touched this time.

It's all so crazy.

But I can tell you what is real
I can tell you what I saw
I saw a hawk and a crow
and then two crows
on the way to you today
And taking you back we saw a hawk
a crow, and then two crows
the same story either way.

And the crows are you and I
at first they fly alone
but then two fly together
into an unknown time.

Please be with me
in your body and your mind
and please hold me
in a way that we will find
that you might love me
given choice, and space, and time

and that I might love you

given choice, and space, and time

Oh you are so beautiful
in your spirit and your face
Come with me woman
to the Garden, through the gates
Back to Nature, that we might revel in Her arms
At one with Nature
as this love grows within our hearts.

Good Omens

Take me away
You did today
Take me away
tomorrow

Watch hawks and crows fly
good omened signs
marking the beginning
of something so special

the Paradoxes and parallels amaze us
you say you remember unknown embraces

Your true face finally shown
the one known to my soul
and the high is a lightness of being.

Hawk and Butterfly

The hawk and the butterfly fly together
together into the unknown
The hawk and the butterfly are so individual
individual, but not alone.

Your path and mine have crossed on purpose
the reason as yet unclear
You and I might go together
into the future so near
you and I might share a home
the tears and joys of love
You and I might share our dream
a dream made strong with hope.

Like Thunder

Sitting here in a daze
don't know what to do or say
You came in like lightning, then left
and it hit me like thunder
all of a sudden, I'm all alone.

Alone...
Knowing where you'll sleep tonight
Knowing that I shouldn't care
But caring.

I told you when I met you
I wasn't good at watching
Someone go from one person to another
It's so damn empty
to see you drive off and leave
being left...
just me, alone.

I like myself fine
But I love being with you.
And you're with him.

It's not my right to know or care

I supposedly fell just three months ago

and she's crying now cause she knows I'm gone

Gone to you

in my mind and in my body

gone to you

but yet I'm all alone.

And you are gone to him

for what?

You say it's dead between you

what about a funeral

A track records of friends

just don't mean shit

if it means I'm living alone

living a lie for months

You told me you would never lie

but from what you say

that's all your life with him is.

Our love I truly treasure

but I'm not sure I can watch you

drive away to him again.

I don't think I can.

After a few month I had to return to California as I had planned all along, to study with Eve and attend Grandfather Raymond's Sweatlodge. When I once more returned east, things between Meagan and myself were unalterably changed. In my absence she had become accidentally, surprisingly pregnant. She never left her man, instead stayed, married him, and raised her child. By now probably many children. I truly hope she rekindled her love and has a happy life.

Be Blessed

The first time I met you
I started reaching out to you
At the time you seemed unhappy
and you were reaching too

But now you smile so brightly
as the child within you grows
and your home life must be happier now
on appearance, it seems so

So forgive me as my hand comes out
I do not mean dishonor
just to act my heart out true

I know your situation
You cannot act upon our feelings
the time for them is past
So I send to you a blessing
as you become a wife
May your child and you be thrice blessed
by Spiritual Love and Light and Life
May your child and you be thrice blessed
by all the joys of Life.

During this period I also wrote a few poems which were commentaries on our culture and times, or were songs to and for the Mother Earth.

I Spit on Progress

I wanted to spit
at the TV
another stupid commercial
telling how their product
had progressed
past all the others...,
it alone was best

Back to back

sparkling with "love"
was another gem
that told people
how to love
it was followed
By Kenney's Shoes
"far out" - "dynamite"

"dynamite progress"
I spit on progress
Progress is the reason why
the rivers can't be drunk from
the reason why
snow turns black
in New York City

and I spit
on fake smiles
and packaged morals
and subtle sexiness
sold on the tube
to subvert your morals
or to comfort you
or to inform you of your deficiencies
which they can fix

or to tell you not to cry tonight
because you didn't score last night

Yeah, TV promises a "good deal"
and a good deal more
Nature's got a good deal more
a good deal more of everything
that's what Natures got
that's what her children have, but wait...
look...
the whales
look quick
they won't be here long
...and then some ingenious
products scientist
will find some new animal to kill
for some exotic ingredient
to make cosmetics with
so people will not have to appear
the way they really are

So now we try as a culture
to convince ourselves
that if we close our eyes
the sins of our self-destruction

will go away
and 29 major animal species
won't be extinct
within twenty years

I spit on progress
if it means
making whales extinct
if it means tearing down
our ancient growth forests
and then planting sawmill trees
only to chop them down
if it means
filling our streams
with chemicals

Then I spit on progress

I spit on progress

If it means the degradation of Nature
If it means the wanton rape of Mother Earth
If progress means these things

Then I spit on progress.

The New Revolution

You know the last revolution
it was killed by drugs and sex
the pendulum swung out way too far
this time, let's work on Peace.

the Old Wave, it has died out
the New Wave has begun
the war we've got to stop this time
is the one man makes on Earth

They put poison on the plants we eat
they say to help them grow
they put poison in the food we buy
they say we like the colors so

Well I think they're damn near crazy
and I think they're going to learn
the Earth has tried to warn us
someday soon we might get burned

In some ways we do deserve it
the way we've dirtied Her
If we had preserved more of her beauty
we'd have never come to this

Are we due for revolution
is it time we purified
will the Air, the Earth, the Water
be purified by Fire?

Well it's time for new beginnings
we're long overdue for change
Mankind must learn to love this planet
if we want to long remain

Yes, we've lost our sense of beauty
we've no temples to the Earth
the lord today is money
will Western culture self-destruct?

I believe the Earth is living
the Mother Earth, she is alive
and if we don't learn to love her soon
it is us that soon will cry

I don't mean to be a prophet
and I don't believe in doom
But I I believe in Nature's Way and Love
and that we've got to wake up soon.

Thy Will be Done

I'm not that high

But I know I need the Light

I know what keeps me safe inside

through the loneliest of nights

I'm not that loving

But I know I need the Love

the Love that keeps you going

Through the fiercest of Life's storms

I'm not that wise

But I know I need the Truth

it's the Truth which sets you free from

those illusions which delude

I'm not that high

But I know I'm going up

I'd rather be evolving

than falling further from the Light

And I've been there

So full of Pride and selfish Greed

a spirit so rebellious

behaving like I was everything

But then I looked to the Creator
the Mother-Father of all Life
and I accepted how She'd made me
Because I know She bore the Light

So I quit rebelling
and took a good look at the Plan
and I know She made me to be me
so I do the best I can

So I try to understand the Way
of the Creator Who made Life
and say "Not my, but Thy Will be done"
every day and every night

And I've got some clues to follow
and one of them is Love
Love is the foundation
Beyond Life, there's only Love.

The Waking Dream

The waking dream is not the true Life

Neither is the sleeping

the true Life is inside and all places

hidden from the dreamer.

The true Life is waiting eons

to become aware of Itself

as the true Life.

Then it takes its place in the true Life

as aware true Life

unchanged

except in knowledge of itself.

The dream is the play of Life.

Base of the Pyramid

To Know - study, thought, introspection, meditation in Nature

To Dare - courage, willingness to change self, to explore the unknown

To Will - to believe, using the ability to direct the forces of Self and Nature to fulfill the desires of the Soul

To be Silent.

Sometimes

Sometimes the wind,

God,

and us

are one.

Sometimes the wind,

God,

and us

are not one.

Part V 1979-1982

By 1979, seven years after the accident, I had come a long way, learned much, and matured some. I was grateful for and appreciative of all my experiences with Eve, and Grandfather Raymond, Dr. Gail, and Ruth Stillman and the others who had guided me on my spiritual journey. Although the healing I had experienced was more spiritual and psychological than physical, I felt healthy and energetic and was ready for something new.

I had spent much of the previous three years with people who were often half a century older than myself; living life primarily through a spiritual framework. I felt that I had lost contact with my own generation and with the cares and concerns of the average person my age.

It was at this point that a long-time acquaintance whom I respected came to me with a business proposition. He said there was a prestigious nightclub for sale in the college town of Athens, Georgia and asked if I was interested in being partners in such an enterprise. I was.

The years 1979 and 1980 were interesting and busy times for me. I was involved in four corporations: one held a patent for an invention, one ran the nightclub, another was helping to start a theater in Atlanta, the other did various investments, and I also played the gold and silver market. Designing and renovating the nightclub was challenging and its opening was very exciting. It was also a very rewarding experience in that during the process of interviewing prospective employees I met the young woman who was to claim my heart for three years.

Carol was a bright-eyed, beautiful freshman majoring in geophysics. She didn't get the waitress job she applied for, she got me instead. I bought a beautiful farm outside Athens, and Carol and I had a wonderful, romantic, passionate relationship. The poems from this time are filled with love and hope.

Quit Asking

It used to be
that every time
I looked into the eyes
of a woman my age
I would ask with my eyes
"Are you the one?"

But lady, since you've come into my life
I've quit asking that question
and we both know why.

Because we've found it
that secret thing called love
because we have it
the miracle of love.

Ain't the Point

Well fucking ain't loving
that ain't the point
love is a sharing
it's not using up
love is a caring
looking out for another
love is a growing
that hurts as its coming.

All I can tell you
is just look around
see what you want
and then make it come down
for all of my losses
and all of my sins
I don't desire it but sacred
Holy Love without end.

I'd Never Seen

Used to see so much wrong
in everything I saw
until I found
I'd never seen

All I ever really looked at
was the anger inside me

Once I felt
the Love outside
and felt it flowing
from within

then I knew what seeing was
for Life and Love is all there is.

The Question

From out of her loving
grey-green eyes
She sparkles a question
to my surprise
A questioned hoped for
but left un-thought
until she finally
asked outright
"Do you want me
as your lady?"

As my lady
to be my lady
Oh sweet love
to be my lady
Yes, if you desire it
I do as well
as long as you
will treat me well
with honesty
and with respect
no catty games
no secret dates

Let's understand
just what we mean
and if to both
it means the same
Then Alright

I am ready
for your love
I am ready
for our love.

Perfect Lover

My perfect lover
Our perfect love
do you see
like I see
how we've both been transformed

We give love
we receive love
with a natural balance
so it seems
Oh, my perfect lover,

This is as good
as it can be

A gift of happiness
a gift of love
it's beyond my belief
just how happy I've become

I never thought
that I'd feel this way
I feel like she's perfect
made just for me

She is my other
my compliment
she is my balance
and my holiness

It scares me I worship
the source of her love
it scares me I'd give her
all that I own

My perfect lover
soon to be perfect wife

we'll be ecstatic
the rest of our life

My perfect lover
my heart's delight
I'll keep you happy
the rest of your life.

Now Is Forever

Right now
we say we'll love each other
forever

Now is Forever

we feel forever and infinity
in a second
we feel the strength
of the Love of Souls
we feel the power
of Spirits shining
we feel the Rightness
the Rightness of Love

I've given my love to you

blessed one

and received yours

with joy and amazement

with joy and amazement

with joy and amazement.

Once More Found

Like the springtime purple flowers
you picked and brought home in a vase
the Light of love that I had lost
is now back in its place.
Like the golden halo of the Moon
coming out behind dark clouds
that trust and honor and sense of Love
that I had lost; I've once more found.

And now it seems that like the fog
Which shrouds what should be seen
your eyes do not convey to you
how much you have healed me.
It's strange that with each passing Sun

and with each passing Moon
Our love appears to grow and deepen
seems no way this love could end.

Mystery of the Goddess

You who are the seed of love
planted in my life
You who are a joyful child
and a woman old and wise
You who showed me many ways
to live a better life
You who gave me confidence
to come back to the Light
You who steal my seed from me
and give me such great pleasure
You who warms my bed at night
and wakes me in the morning
You who bring me ecstasy
and the Mystery of the Goddess
You who brought true love to me
shall have my love forever.

As always happens, as time goes on, instead of being lost in love and imagining your partner is the answer to all your wants and needs, you begin to see things more the way they really are. This always happens, after awhile some sense of reality sets in.

So Mean

It may be all the hurt I've had
that makes me so damn mean
but our love, like a Georgia Monsoon
seems a rain that washes clean

The growing pains of our young love
come and go, yet our love stays
the edges that were rough, get smoothed
at some price along the way

All the fights and all the fuss
and the times that we forget
are as nothing beside the love and joy
that together we create.

That first year with Carol was the fulfillment of so many dreams. We had a lovely home and farm, and the nightclub was time consuming, and at first, interesting work.

Our first spring we went on vacation to St. Lucia in the Caribbean. We took Tom with us so he could visit his girlfriend, now his wife, Debbie, who was working in the Peace Corps there.

I was doing things I'd dreamed of, and had the kind of relationship I'd longed for. It was a wonderful time to be young, alive, and in love. The first year, maybe two were great. Then, grabbing defeat from the jaws of victory, things began to fall apart. As time went on competition from much larger clubs with more buying power cut into our business. The Jimmy Carter Inflation/Recession hurt me economically and jacked my floating mortgage way up. I became overextended economically, mentally, and physically. Carol's studies became more demanding and her drive and ambition required her to spend long hours studying. Our schedules grew to be so different we had little time together. A relationship is like any living thing, it needs to be nurtured. It seemed like we didn't have any time to nurture our relationship. The night life began to wear on me and I began drinking immoderately and snorting some of the cocaine floating around the club scene.

As business got worse, the economy continued to slide towards chaos, the gold and silver markets collapsed, my drinking and cocaine use became excessive, and my relationship with Carol became more and more strained. Carol and I had talked in general terms about our future together and marriage, but there were some obvious logistical problems. She was very ambitious and motivated and would not stop short of a Ph.D. and a career in geophysics which would eventually entail considerable traveling and extended separations. We were reaching a point of make-it or break-it, we were either going to commit the rest of our lives to each other, or break free and go our separate ways.

Impaired by the haze of alcohol abuse, inflamed by excessive cocaine use, while stone drunk and out of my mind, I pulled a self-destruct on our relationship and found a cheater's bed. Although there is constant sexual temptation in the night life, my actions were not conscious, I was just dead drunk. Carol caught me cold. She was deeply hurt and felt betrayed. I felt incredibly guilty about it all, and very hypocritical, as well I should have. I hadn't lived up to my own morals or expectations. I betrayed her and failed myself. I had done what Peggy had done to me, with the exception that mine was one night of infidelity, not a year or more of deception.

In repeated periods of introspection I tried to figure out some reason or motive for my actions. All I could come up with was that I must have subconsciously wanted to be free but consciously loved her too much to let go. There was a problematic future due to her career choices, would I follow her around as she pursued her career, or would there be extended separations? Due to the economy, the club, and my growing alcohol and cocaine abuse problems, our relationship had hit very rough roads before the cheating incident. I must have intentionally, if unconsciously, pulled the self-destruct on the relationship. My guilt over my short-sightedness and hurtful behavior was soul crushing, and losing Carol while my business was failing was personally devastating. My alcohol and cocaine abuse only worsened.

I made repeated attempts to explain to Carol my failure to be loyal and my self-abusive behaviors. I was trying to explain it to her, as well as myself. Who really knows why a person would ruin the best chance for happiness he had ever had?

I had experienced some bad luck before, but I had never really failed at anything. Just as many people have gone bankrupt during the 2009-10 recession, I was financially ruined by the Jimmy Carter recession. I got over-extended and could never make it back. The failure of my nightclub and my other economic endeavors, my inability to become liquid and solvent, my failure to live up to my own moral standards, and my failure to stay straight and sober despite the obvious ill effects of such behavior - all preyed upon my mind.

The poems from this period reflect the dark state of mind I found myself in, and my attempt to search for reason and meaning in the midst of what seemed like multiple catastrophes. But as I have so often found in Life, it seems we learn more during the difficult and challenging times than when everything is rosy.

I Step Willingly Into the Darkness

I step willingly into the Darkness
Blind, unseeing
But trusting in the Unknown Peril
too long in the Light.
I step willingly into the Darkness

unseeing and unafraid.

The Light that was our Love
would have choked me
with the stagnation of our Happiness.
I knew naught, but joyful surrender
to the Fiery Passion of our Love
Letting it fill me and take me
Strangling the awareness of myself
Losing to the identity of our Shared Being.

I step willingly into the Darkness
losing the Light that for years
Kept me safe, Chained far away
from the reality of my Shadow.

I step Boldly into the Darkness
challenging the Light of our Love
with the Darkness of Isolation
Shattering the Core, Exploding the Shell
Leaving our Love, or lack of it
to face the naked humanity
of ourselves, our lives, our pretensions.

I step Blindly into the Darkness

carrying the shield of Isolation
seeking the consoling pains of loneliness
of that Divine Desperation
that causes seeking of the Farthest Shores
for that which is most deeply hidden

Sleeping.

I Step Willingly into the Darkness
I Step Blindly into the Darkness
I Step Boldly into the Darkness

Trusting, Waiting, Hoping.

One Hundred Hunters

Always in the Late, Late Evening
Only in the Chill of Nighttime
Only through the veils of Darkness
it stalks me like One Hundred Hunters.

Waiting, Watching is the lioness
for the prey to walk too closely

to the Jaws of Death wide open
Waiting, Watching, never flinching
Never gives Herself Away.
Like a deer with eyes wide open
Always watching, Always hoping
I the Fool do tread too closely
to the Jaws of my destruction
oblivious to the scent of Pain.
She Pounces Quickly, Deathly, Silent
Ripping, Tearing to my core
And I alone, a Child of Darkness
feel her teeth as they close home.

And yet One Hundred Hunters waiting
Find that I am still alone
Embraced so tightly by the Beauty
of the Pain my Heart made home.
I the Deer, and I the Lioness
God - One Hundred Hunters Watching
Loneliness is my salvation
and Pain a friend who always comes.

And so the Night moves on till Morning
and I alone shall sit here Mourning
waiting, watching for the dawning

when the Light shall slay the Darkness
to find me still the same, embattled,
Soul oppressed by a weight unbearable
This pain that will not die.

Stop the Wind

It's hoping against a tragic ending
in a movie that ends sad
it's grabbing a handful of blowing sand
or trying to stop the wind

it's knowing time just keeps on going
and forgetting half your dreams
it's sitting on the sidelines watching
waiting to go in

It's all the pain in the here and now
that doesn't go away
it's watching children grow up quickly
and parents go away

it's all the tears I want to cry
that won't run down my face

it's all the crazy things I do
that don't make sense to me

I've nourished all my life a dream
that I could do it all
that the things they claimed impossible
I could overcome

But I can't stop the blowing wind
or grab sand from the air
I can't bring dead parents back
or recall forgotten dreams

But still I hold on to the thought
that sometimes sleeps in me
that I will do those things I want
that I'll live out my dreams

But I can't stop this river running
that wells up in my soul
it's sad and lonely in this world
when you're sitting all alone

When you realize that you will not fulfill
the hopes and dreams you've had

but that you are just another sad person

trying to stop the wind.

Queen of Hearts

I had been so lonely so long

all I had was hope

But then I found the Queen of Hearts

which is the Queen of Cups

the Queen of Cups is faithful love

come from a good wife

We both had a year so happy

I didn't need the Light.

But sunrise come and sunset go

and all there is must change

the Mystery was not so strong

nor was our minds' exchange

You had your great ambition

and the studies they required

I had an Albatross of a business

it's sale my one desire

So sunset went and nighttime came

I found a cheater's bed

and you decided there and then

there'd be no second chance.
And sunrise come and sunset go
and I feel so alone
I then found the Three of Spades
of course, the Three of Swords
three swords through a broken heart
a loved one gone away
You still have your great ambition
and I an Albatross to slay
But ambition will not keep you warm
in the winter nights to come
and my Albatross will be long dead and gone
before I forget our love.

Butterfly Flying Free

She's becoming a free and independent woman
a butterfly flying free
with good memories of a warm cocoon
and crystal blue skies which wait
the sadness does not hold her back
her loss is not that great
for love, once found, is slow to die
and often hides and waits.

Strong and Silent

I must be quiet and stand aside
and let you walk out of my life
I must be strong and silent, still
while part of my heart cries

All the joy that I had known
fades as you pull away
all the warmth of the home we made
like your love, just drains away
all that is in me starts to rebel
to proclaim that you must stay
but it's my own failings that has brought this end
for my sins I stand sentenced to pain.

Newness Fades

There's too much hurt to turn back
and pick up the pieces again
there's too many times we can't believe
what each other said
the dream of newness fades away
as fog does from the sun

and bit by bit our once shining love
is revealed with all its flaws
although what we had was good and real
we didn't see things the same
and now we stand so far apart
not even the passion remains
but physical love would not be enough
to make either of us stay
in a situation born of lies
lies and all my shame
we should have had
what could have been
but now that's torn apart
I hope Time will leave us with happy memories
and let the bad ones be forgot.

Hold on to the Future

Every time I see you
it's just the same inside
I want you and I love you
and I want to run and cry
I hurt you and I shamed you
I behaved so wrong

now I'm trying, feel like dying
cause I can't bring you home.
I wonder if you love me now
or how much you ever did
did you love me like I loved you
when we were happy way back when
and if you really felt the way
I thought that we both did
will you hold on to some future hope
that we might feel that way again?

Stuffed Monkey

She kept the stuffed monkey
we both got our records back
she kept the jewelry that I bought her
and I kept my lion's head ring

She is older now, and wiser
I was part of one sad lesson taught
she learned not to take a heart for granted
I found I wasn't ready for a wife

There was so much love and happiness

at first
there was ecstasy and joy
there were bright eyes
shining in the darkness
and pleasure like we'd never known.

The pre- and post-breakup periods, and the extended period it took me to sell my nightclub were dark times. Sometimes the poems were dark comments on my self-abuse. I felt I had been blessed by many wonderful spiritual experiences, and I was abysmally aware that I wasn't living up to what I'd been taught. Although at the time I had no fear that I would be trapped in such behavior forever and I felt it was just a dark period I was passing through; the drinking and cocaine abuse brought about a feeling of a loss of self-worth and brought on self-loathing.

Dark Stage Passing

Well I put myself to sleep now
every night that I'm alone
I smoke my way or I drink my way
Just as long as my eyes close
don't care too much about what I do

how I act or what I say

as long as I can slip away

at the end of every day.

I've been drinking too much, way too much

off and on sixteen years

I've tried some different drugs, it's true

going on for thirteen years

and I don't know yet just what it is

that I hide or shun

I don't know if it's me that's looking

or me I run away from.

Well I'm drunk when it turns nighttime

and I'm sick when it turns light

I'm trying to kill this pain inside

but it's growing worse with time

I just cannot forget our love

though I threw it all away

threw away a true love

on a stupid barroom fling.

I don't want all these damn habits

I don't want to be a drunk

but every time I find I'm sober

it's time to run amuck

I can't forget, forget our love

though I threw it all away
threw away a true love
on a stupid barroom fling.

All my friends are really worried
never seen me down so low
they just shake their heads and wonder
just how far down I'm gonna go
But I can't forget, forget our love
can't believe the mindless waste
to throw away a good true love
on a stupid barroom fling.

Well I'm living in my mind now
but I cloud it over good
I was living in my balls for a while
but it didn't do no good
and I can't go back and change the past
it's no good to even try
but this sadness ain't no good for me
these damn dark clouds just block the Light.

I keep thinking about my lifetime
I keep thinking about the past
keep worrying when the bill collector

gonna demand his cash

and I can't get straight, I can't stay straight

I can't go on like this

but this is just a dark stage passing

I'll hear Life's sweet call again.

Stopped Feeling Young

I stopped feeling young this year

    though I still have all the dreams

that I nurtured as a child

they're still alive inside of me

So I lost another love

one I really needed to keep

once I'd thrown it all away

I realized what she'd meant to me

I don't much like this growing up

    or living without a love

in the mirror it's not me anymore

the face is old and way too scared

so now what about all those dreams

the ones I wanted to come true
I was going to have a wife and home
peace and happiness, love too

Well I'm all grown up it seems
but it's just not like I thought
it's not happy ever after
God - it's not happy here at all

I stopped feeling young this year
I stopped feeling much at all
if it weren't for will and faith and hope
I wouldn't have made it for this long

I watched some loved ones leave this year
back to Heaven so they say
some were ready, so it seemed
others weren't, left anyway
Yeah I quit feeling young this year
I quit feeling much at all
there's no happy ever after
there's just will and faith and hope.

Just Like Them

I didn't think that it could happen
to a Nature-freak like me
I'm far away from the Goddess now
like a baby that needs feeding
I had seen it all my lifetime
and had pitied one and all
who were so tied up in business
they saw no changes spring to fall
And now it seems I'm like them
those I despised so much in youth
I'm cut off from my roots in Her
got to get back with Mother Earth
And God I've gotten sick again
been sick too much this spring
I've been four months on the wagon
just can't seem to find relief
I feel fingers pulling at my soul
taking just a little, but enough
to leave my aura shattered still
Lord God I've had enough

Some say it's the peyote
some say it's my mind

some say it was her cooking
some say it's my ex-wife
some say it's too much cocaine
that has numbed me through and through
some say it's been too many nights
drunk and on the loose
some say it's way too many days
I sat in dark cafes
drinking, drinking, and watching girls
girls and women play

But I don't think those things are it
they're the symptoms and the pain
but they are not the illness' cause
just its results along the way

The illness is an isolation
I'm cut off from Her blood
that runs up from the Heart of Her
Whom well I once did serve

Some say it's a passing thing
some say it's going to stay
some say I'll live a hundred years
but the odds say too few days

But I've got to get on home now
to the womb of Mother Earth
if she'll give me Her sweet breast once more
I'll no longer feel this lost
and if I just can feel again
the natural wonder of a child
I'll find the balance that I need
to not get lost this time.

After a bad, dark, reckless, dangerous period, I finally sold my nightclub, farm, and North Carolina cabin, all at huge losses. I returned to Atlanta to go back to college and start over. It was time to get the monkeys off my back, climb off my self-made cross, and get back to Life again. It wasn't going to happen overnight.

Child of Freedom

Just before she set me free
Love, she came and said to me
Love is all you'll ever need
but child, keep hold of Freedom

Life will take you by surprise

women, they can change their minds
people change, some even lie
sometimes for no good reason

But Love, she said, can set you free
you're the one you really need
learn to love yourself and be
one who stands for Freedom.

C - Section of the Soul

I've been in labor half my life
waiting on the "new me" to be born
And if I don't give spiritual birth real soon
it will be a c - section of the soul

I'm the surgeon, and the mother
and I pick up the knife
I've died and died so many times
now or never - rebirth strikes.

Still the lessons taught by Jesus
or shown by St. Germane
are what I need or so I thought

but still, I laugh again

I laugh and laugh and hold my side
as laughter overflows
I don't know exactly what I want
just the re-birth of my soul.

www.ingramcontent.com/pod-product-compliance
Lightning Source LLC
Chambersburg PA
CBHW080448170426
43196CB00016B/2728